Eat Your Way To Success And Learn How To Control Hunger - A Weight Loss Surgery Friendly Cookbook

Edie,
Good luck as
you begin your
new journey & stay
Have fun
healthy
new life!
through your
Jodi

Edie -
My hope is that this cookbook
finds a forever home in your kitchen.
Always remember that protein
+ produce
SUCCESS!
Sincerely
Wendy

Eat Your Way To Success And Learn How To Control Hunger - A Weight Loss Surgery Friendly Cookbook

Wendy Campbell & Sandi Henderson

Disclaimer

The recipes in this book have been created by weight loss surgery patients for weight loss surgery patients and their families. While reasonable attempts have been made to provide reliable directions and correct nutritional values, WLS Success Matters disclaims any responsibility for accuracy.

WLS Success Matters encourages each of you to be personally accountable for your choices regarding your meal plans and adhering to the nutritional guidelines provided to you by your bariatric team.

WLS Success Matters specifically disclaims all responsibility for any liability, loss, or risk, personal or otherwise, that is incurred as a consequence of the use or application of any of the material in this book.

Published by WLS Success Matters, LLC
P.O. Box 1389
Ventura, CA 93002
www.wlssuccessmatters.com

ISBN-10: 153972879X
ISBN-13: 9781539728795
Library of Congress Control Number: 2016918035
CreateSpace Independent Publishing Platform
North Charleston, South Carolina

Contents

Preface

WELCOME TO *Eat Your Way to Success and Learn How to Control Hunger*. What you will find on the pages to follow are recipes with **real food**, **real nutrition**, and **easy-to-follow directions**. We've created this book in response to thousands of inquiries about what each of us has chosen to eat after bariatric surgery to reach our healthy weight and to maintain it for a lifetime. With almost twenty years' experience between us in 2016, we have achieved a level of health neither of us had thought possible before weight loss surgery.

These are just a few of the things we know to be true:

- Learning how to eat is necessary for long-term weight loss surgery success.
- New ideas are helpful.
- Successful, healthy people live in routines with plans in place for daily living.
- Be sure to put only the bariatric portion on your plate.
- Cooking in batches, with repeat meals for breakfast and lunch, frequently takes the difficulty out of wondering, "What will I eat next?"
- Accessing resources at your fingertips in today's world can support your success.

You, the patient, are the one accountable for what and how much is going on your plate. Let us be the pages you turn next to find your success.

In our cookbook, we include the core principles that the majority of bariatric centers advise patients to use as their nutritional guidelines for food choices. We eat protein first and include fresh produce in our meals.

Our hope is that by trying the recipes in this book that we and our friends and family have enjoyed, you will be able to create some of your own kitchen miracles. It doesn't matter if you're short on time, live alone, don't know how to cook, or don't believe you are a good cook; there are recipes that let you throw the ingredients in a pan and have a meal done in twenty minutes, and there are others that you just toss into a slow cooker in the morning and then come home to dinner ready to serve. It's all real food made by you for you and your family to enjoy! Happy belly, happy mind!

If you have any questions or doubts about what your bariatric center's recommendations might be, don't hesitate to pick up the phone and ask them. That's what we would do.

These recipes are a collection of some of our personal favorites. They have been liked, shared, and tried by our friends in social media and by clients around the globe. May they provide you the flavor explosions and foodie satisfaction that we have enjoyed.

Now start eating your way to success!

Wendy & Sandi

Breakfasts

BREAKFAST SETS THE tone for your day. Prior to weight loss surgery, we both frequently skipped breakfast as part of "diet" routines to help with weight loss. As weight loss surgery patients, we learned that breakfast, and especially the protein we get at that meal, is necessary to kick-start our metabolism and our day. We have both found that having breakfast repeats work. Whether this means having prepared breakfasts in the refrigerator or freezer or planning your breakfasts for the week ahead is up to you.

5-Minute On-Point Breakfast

Mr. C likes to top this one off with habanero salsa.

Ingredients:

- 2 links Al Fresco chicken sausage
- 1 egg
- 2 tablespoons nonfat milk
- 1 teaspoon minced garlic
- ¼ cup shredded light Mexican cheese
- Salt and pepper, to taste
- ¼ teaspoon Trader Joe's 21 Seasoning Salute (you can use Mrs. Dash® Table Blend as well)
- Crushed red pepper, to taste (if you dare!)

Directions:

1. Microwave sausage for 2 minutes per package directions.
2. Spray large glass measuring cup with nonstick cooking spray.
3. Add egg, milk, garlic, cheese, salt, pepper, seasoning, and crushed red pepper (if you dare). Whisk well.
4. Place measuring cup with egg mixture in microwave and cook for 90 seconds. Remove and whisk.
5. Place measuring cup with egg mixture back in microwave and cook for another 90 seconds. Remove, stir, and serve with sausage.

Nutrition: Makes 1 serving.

- 250 calories
- 26 grams protein

Baked Egg Cups

The recipe calls for a dozen eggs and a muffin tin with twelve openings; this will certainly feed a group! Feel free to reduce the recipe down to the size you need. These little cups are *super easy* to make and are packed with protein and a cheesy flair.

Ingredients:

- 12 eggs
- 12 thin slices of deli ham (round)
- ½ cup grated Parmesan cheese (or your favorite cheese)
- ½ cup diced scallions
- Freshly cracked sea salt and pepper

Directions:

1. Preheat oven to 400 degrees.
2. Spray muffin tin with nonstick cooking spray.
3. Lay one piece of ham in each hole, creating a little ham cup.
4. Crack one egg into each hole.
5. Sprinkle with salt and pepper.
6. Bake eggs for about 12 minutes, until whites are firm and yolks are still nice and runny. Bake longer if you want firmer yolks.
7. Carefully remove each egg from muffin tin.
8. Top with grated cheese and scallions.

Nutritional Data: Makes 12 servings (1 egg cup per serving). Each serving has:

- 100 calories
- 18 grams protein

Blended Mocha Protein

The best of both worlds: coffee and protein. It will jump-start your day!

Ingredients:

- 1 cup brewed coffee
- ½ scoop Isopure Dutch Chocolate protein powder (or your favorite chocolate protein powder)
- 2 tablespoons unsweetened cashew milk (or your favorite nut milk)
- 1 packet Splenda (or your choice of zero-calorie sweetener)
- Handful Ice
- 2 tablespoons fat-free whipped topping

Directions:

1. Pour coffee over ice.
2. Mix protein powder, milk, and Splenda in separate cup. Use fork to mix and break up all clumps.
3. Pour protein mix over iced coffee.
4. Add mixture to blender and blend on high for 1 minute.
5. Pour into tall glass and add whipped topping.

Nutrition: Makes 1 serving.

- 86.1 calories
- 12.5 grams protein

Blueberry Peanut Butter Chocolate Protein Shake

Great shake on the way to the gym. You can add one tablespoon of flax seed meal for the omega-3s and the fiber to keep things moving. If you add flax to your shake, remember to add the extra calories to the total.

Ingredients:

- 1 scoop Isoflex peanut butter chocolate protein powder
- 1 tablespoon PB2 powdered peanut butter
- ½ cup frozen blueberries
- ½ cup almond milk
- Ice cubes and water

Directions:

1. Place all ingredients in blender.
2. Blend on high and enjoy.

Nutrition: Makes one serving.

- 200 calories
- 30 grams protein

Blueberry Ricotta Power Cakes

Weekends allow for "special" breakfasts that take a little extra time to prepare. These power cakes are just that—delicious, packed with protein, fiber, and antioxidants, and worth the time to prepare. They are great without butter or syrup since the ricotta cheese and blueberries make them sweet enough.

Ingredients:

- 1 cup Kodiak Cakes Power Cakes Flapjack and Waffle Mix
- 1 cup nonfat milk
- ½ cup nonfat ricotta cheese
- 2 egg whites
- ¼ cup water
- ¾ cup blueberries

Directions:

1. In large bowl, mix all ingredients except blueberries together. Whisk, making sure ricotta is well blended into batter.
2. Gently fold in blueberries.
3. Spray two 8-inch frying pans with nonstick cooking spray and place on stove over medium-low to medium heat.
4. Pour about ¼ cup batter into each pan and cook until edges of pancakes are dry and tops are bubbly.
5. Flip pancakes over and cook on other side for about 1 minute.
6. Transfer cooked pancake to another plate (keep your plates warm in a 200-degree oven and transfer the cooked pancakes to these plates).

7. Repeat cooking process until all batter is used. Spray pans as needed.
8. Serve and enjoy!

Nutrition: Makes three servings.
Each serving approximately has:

- 228 calories
- 20 grams protein

BW's Breakfast Parfait

Great to serve to guests or even as a simple supper on a hot summer evening.

Ingredients:

- 6 ounces nonfat plain Fage Greek yogurt, divided
- ½ cup Special K Protein cereal, divided
- ¼ medium banana, sliced thin
- 1 packet Splenda (or your choice of zero-calorie sweetener), divided
- ½ kiwi, chopped
- ¼ cup blueberries
- 1 tablespoon glazed walnut pieces

Directions:

1. Start assembly with empty wine glass.
2. Build your parfait in layers:
   - First layer: ½ of yogurt, ¼ cup cereal, banana, and sprinkle of Splenda
   - Second layer: other ½ of yogurt, ¼ cup cereal, kiwi, sprinkle of Splenda
   - Third layer: blueberries, rest of Splenda, then walnut pieces

Nutrition: Makes 1 serving.

- 290 calories
- 27.7 grams protein

Cherry-Vanilla Cheese Bowl

This is like eating a bowl of cherry-vanilla ice cream for breakfast or lunch.

Quick, easy, protein packed, and satisfying.

Ingredients:

- ½ cup low-fat cottage cheese
- ¼ cup fat-free ricotta cheese
- 1 teaspoon vanilla
- ⅓ cup frozen pitted dark cherries
- 1 teaspoon lemon or lime juice
- 2 tablespoons Splenda (or your choice of zero-calorie sweetener)

Directions:

1. In small bowl, mix together cottage cheese, ricotta cheese, and vanilla. Set aside.
2. In microwave-safe measuring cup or bowl, mix together cherries, lemon juice, and Splenda. Microwave on 50 percent power for about 1 minute. Remove and break up cherries with fork. Microwave on 50 percent power for another 15 seconds. Stir together and pour over cheese mixture. Enjoy!

Nutrition: Makes 1 serving.

- 193 calories
- 20.5 grams protein

Chile Relleno Casserole

It's great for breakfast, lunch, or dinner. Make it on Sunday, cut it into eight pieces, and wrap and store them in the fridge. It makes it easy to pop them into the microwave during the week for breakfast or lunch.

Ingredients:

- 1 (27 ounce) can whole green chilies
- 2 (7 ounce) bags Kraft fat-free shredded cheddar cheese
- 32 ounces Egg Beaters (egg substitute)
- Salsa (optional)

Directions:

1. Preheat oven to 350 degrees.
2. Spray a 9 x 13-inch pan with olive oil or coconut oil spray.
3. Place half of chilies in single layer in pan.
4. Top with shredded cheese.
5. Repeat with second layer.
6. Pour Egg Beaters over chile-cheese layers.
7. Bake for about 40 minutes or until center is just set.
8. Enjoy with or without salsa.

Nutrition: Makes 8 servings.
Each serving approximately has:

- 165 calories
- 28 grams protein

Cinnamon Roll Protein Shake

All the flavor you love minus the fat and calories. Boom!

Ingredients:

- ¼ cup oats
- 1 tablespoon brown sugar
- ¼ teaspoon cinnamon
- ½ medium banana
- 1 cup unsweetened cashew milk (or your favorite nut milk)
- 1 scoop Isopure Creamy Vanilla Protein Powder (or your favorite vanilla protein powder)
- Handful ice

Directions:

1. Put all ingredients into blender.
2. Blend on high for 2 minutes.
3. Pour over ice, sip, and enjoy!

Nutrition: Makes 1 serving.

- 313 calories
- 31 grams protein

Craig's Ham and Egg Scramble

An excellent way to use up leftover ham from the holidays.

Ingredients:

- 3 ounces cooked ham, chopped
- 1 teaspoon minced garlic
- 1 egg
- 2 tablespoons nonfat milk
- ¼ cup shredded light Mexican cheese
- Salt and pepper, to taste
- ¼ teaspoon Trader Joe's 21 Seasoning Salute (you can use Mrs. Dash® Table Blend as well)
- Crushed red pepper, to taste (if you dare!)
- ¼ teaspoon Johnny's Garlic Spread and Seasoning (or any brand garlic seasoning)

Directions:

1. Spray skillet with nonstick cooking spray.
2. Turn heat to high, and add ham and garlic to skillet. Sautee until ham starts to get crispy.
3. In small bowl, combine egg, milk, cheese, salt and pepper, seasoning, crushed red pepper (if desired), and garlic seasoning. Whisk together and then add to skillet.
4. Stir to scramble and cook egg mixture. It will cook fast. When egg is cooked, remove from heat and eat.

Nutrition: Makes 1 serving.

- 305 calories
- 33 grams protein

Cream Cheese and Lox Omelet

Childhood memories of Sunday morning breakfasts inspired the birth of this cream cheese and "lox" omelet for two. Try it! It's yummy, protein packed, and sure to please if this is your style.

Ingredients:

- 4 ounces smoked salmon
- 4 tablespoons fat-free cream cheese
- 1 egg
- 5 egg whites

Directions:

1. Spray 10-inch skillet with nonstick cooking spray (a current favorite is coconut oil spray—*nothing* sticks to it). Preheat over medium heat.
2. Pull salmon apart with fork into small bits and then warm it in microwave for 10–15 seconds on 50 percent power. Set aside.
3. Warm cream cheese in microwave on 50 percent power for 5 seconds (so it will distribute easily over eggs).
4. Whisk egg and egg whites together and pour into preheated skillet.
5. Cook egg mixture until it is almost fully set.
6. Add salmon and then cream cheese over half of egg mixture and carefully fold other half over filling.
7. Cook until omelet is thoroughly warm, eggs are completely cooked, and cream cheese has started to melt (toss a drop of water in the pan and then cover it so the omelet steams).
8. Slide onto plate, cut in half, and serve with sliced tomatoes if you like.

Alternative Directions:

Cook egg mixture until almost set, and then add salmon and cream cheese over entire pan. Cover and finish cooking.

Nutrition: Makes 2 servings.
Each serving approximately has:

- 200 calories
- 30.5 grams protein

Full of It Protein Shake

This combo helps keep your gut happy and your days regular.
wink
Your body will thank you!

Ingredients:

- 2 cups ice, divided
- ½ medium banana
- 8 ounces unsweetened cashew milk
- 1 tablespoon ground flax seed
- 2 tablespoons PB2 powdered peanut butter
- 1 cup spinach leaves
- 1 scoop of Isopure Dutch Chocolate 100 percent whey isolate protein powder

Directions:

1. Add 1 cup ice to blender.
2. Add banana, cashew milk, flax seed, powdered peanut butter, spinach, and protein powder.
3. Blend on high for 2 minutes.
4. Add rest of ice to 20-ounce cup.
5. Pour blended mixture over ice and enjoy.

Nutrition: Makes 1 serving.

- 246 calories
- 31.6. grams protein

Italian Job Omelet

If you hadn't noticed, we love eggs and egg substitute and creating new and tasty omelet sensations. Here's one with just a few ingredients and loads of flavor.

Ingredients:

- ½ cup egg substitute
- 6 slices Gallo Lite Dry Salame, chopped
- 1 ounce Trader Joe's Shredded Lite Mozzarella Cheese
- 2 tablespoons Trader Joe's Bruschetta Sauce

Directions:

1. Spray an 8-inch skillet with nonstick cooking spray. Heat pan over medium heat.
2. Pour egg substitute into pan.
3. Cover and allow egg to almost set (about 3 to 4 minutes—watch it carefully).
4. Add chopped salame and cheese to cover half of egg mixture, then flip other half over to cover filling. Allow omelet to set completely, until cheese melts (1–2 minutes max).
5. Slide out of pan onto plate, top with bruschetta sauce, and enjoy.

Nutrition: Makes 1 serving.

- 165 calories
- 21.5 grams protein

Northwest Meets Southwest Omelet

It was time that some salmon met some Hatch green chiles.
That's all!

Ingredients:

- 2 eggs
- 4 egg whites
- 6 tablespoons chopped Hatch green chilies
- 2 ounces smoked sockeye salmon, flaked
- 2 ounces Trader Joe's Lite Shredded Mozzarella Cheese

Directions:

1. Spray 10-inch skillet with nonstick cooking spray.
2. Heat skillet over medium or medium-high heat.
3. In small bowl, whisk together eggs and egg whites.
4. Pour into pan and cover. Cook until almost set (watch carefully—your pan type and stovetop will determine the time—perhaps 2 minutes).
5. Add chilies, salmon, and cheese to cover half of egg mixture and fold other half of cooked egg mixture over filling.
6. Cover and cook for about another minute or until cheese is just melted.
7. Remove from heat, slide onto plate, and serve.

Nutrition: Makes 2 servings.
Each serving approximately has:

- 225 calories
- 25 grams protein

Orange Protein Pancakes

A little orange zest goes a long way into making a delightful and protein-rich breakfast treat. Your family can add butter and syrup to theirs or eat them just as they come off the skillet. Yummy!

Ingredients:

- 2 small bananas
- 1 egg
- 8 egg whites
- Zest of 1 orange
- 1 teaspoon cinnamon
- 1 teaspoon vanilla

Directions:

1. Place all ingredients in blender and blend until smooth.
2. Spray skillet with nonstick cooking spray (coconut oil spray works well) and heat skillet over medium-high heat (you can keep two small skillets going).
3. Pour in about ¼ cup of batter and cook until edges of pancakes begin to dry and bubbles appear in center.
4. Flip pancakes and cook for about a minute on other side.
5. Remove pancakes to plate and cover to keep warm, or keep warm in a 150- to 200-degree oven.
6. Serve and enjoy!

PRO-TIP: Add one slice uncured Canadian bacon to your plate for an additional 20 calories and 3.7 grams protein.

Nutrition: Makes 4 servings.
Each serving has approximately:

- 89 calories
- 7.5 grams protein

Pastrami and Swiss Cheese—Not on Rye Bread

Trader Joe's once again made it possible to enjoy an old favorite deli meal—pastrami and swiss. Just how did they do that? They now have uncured pastrami that is as lean as can be, and two ounces of it has only 100 calories and 15 grams of protein. Add some of TJ's Jarlsberg Lite Reduced-Fat Swiss Cheese and some deli mustard, and it's heavenly.

Ingredients:

- 3 ounces Trader Joe's pastrami
- 2 tablespoons water
- 1 egg
- 5 egg whites
- 1 slice Trader Joe's Jarlsberg Lite Reduced Fat Swiss cheese, cut into strips
- Deli mustard, if desired

Directions:

1. Lightly spray 10-inch skillet with nonstick cooking spray. Heat skillet, and place pastrami in pan with 2 tablespoons of water. Cover and let steam for 1 minute.
2. Stir, then cover for another minute until water evaporates and pastrami is thoroughly heated. Remove pastrami from pan. Spray skillet again.
3. Whisk together egg and egg whites (add a drop of water to this) and pour into prepared skillet over medium heat.
4. Cover and cook eggs until almost set.
5. Add pastrami first, and then add strips of cheese to cover half of egg mixture.

6. With spatula, fold half of egg mixture to cover pastrami and cheese.
7. Turn heat to low, add a few drops of water to pan, and cover. Cook omelet until eggs are set and cheese is melted.
8. Slide onto plate, cut in half with spatula, top with deli mustard (if desired), and enjoy.

Nutrition: Makes two servings.
Each serving has approximately:

- 180 calories
- 27.25 grams protein

Peanut Butter Lovers Protein Shake

All the yumminess of peanut butter minus the fat and calories.
Pump it up with coffee if you so choose.

Ingredients:

- 2 tablespoons PB2 powdered peanut butter
- 1 cup ice
- ½ cup unsweetened cashew milk (or your favorite nut milk)
- ½ medium banana
- 1 scoop Isopure Creamy Vanilla Protein Powder (or your favorite vanilla protein powder)
- ¼ cup iced coffee, if desired

Directions:

1. Add all ingredients to blender.
2. Blend on high for 2 minutes.
3. Pour over more ice. Sip and enjoy the peanut butter dream!

Nutrition: Makes 1 serving.

- 214.5 calories
- 31 grams protein

Sexy Greek Berries
Food does not get sexier than this!

Ingredients:

- 1 large strawberry, diced
- ½ cup blackberries
- 2 packets of Splenda (or your choice of zero-calorie sweetener)
- 1 cup plain nonfat Greek yogurt

Directions:

1. Heat berries and Splenda in microwave for 1 minute.
2. Spoon yogurt into small bowl.
3. Pour heated berry mixture over yogurt.

Nutrition: Makes one serving.

- 157 calories
- 22.5 grams protein

Vanilla and Chocolate Twist Shake

This is like the twisted soft-serve cone we had as kids.

Ingredients:

- ¾ cup ice
- 8 ounces unsweetened cashew milk (or any nut milk you prefer)
- 1 tablespoon PB2 powdered peanut butter with chocolate
- 1 tablespoon cookies-and-cream pudding mix
- ½ scoop Isopure 100 percent Whey Creamy Vanilla Protein Powder (or any vanilla protein powder)
- ½ scoop Isopure 100 percent Whey Dutch Chocolate Protein Powder (or any chocolate protein powder)

Directions:

1. Put all ingredients into blender.
2. Blend on high for 2 minutes.
3. Pour over more ice, sip, and enjoy!

Nutrition: Makes 1 serving.

- 215 calories
- 27 grams protein

Lunches

LUNCH GETS SQUEEZED into our busy days and needs to be protein-centric, quick, simple, and frequently grab-and-go. Both of us have found that preparing lunches in advance and having grab-and-go items within reach help us feed our hunger *and* stay on track.

Three Countries Meet for Lunch Together

A little bit of Italy, a little bit of Germany, and dash of Canada make for a lot of taste.

Ingredients:

- 3 slices Jarlsberg light swiss cheese
- 9 slice Jones uncured Canadian bacon
- 2 teaspoons Trader Joe's Aioli Garlic Mustard Sauce
- Toothpicks

Directions:

1. Cover baking sheet with foil and spray lightly with nonstick cooking spray.
2. Preheat oven to 450 degrees.
3. Cut each cheese slice into 3 equal pieces.
4. On foil-covered baking sheet, stack one Canadian bacon slice, tiny dollop of mustard, and ⅓ cheese slice. Roll and pierce with toothpick to hold rollup together.
5. Repeat until all 9 are done.
6. Place in oven for about 5 minutes or until cheese is melted.
7. Serve and enjoy!

Nutrition: Makes 3 servings.
Each serving has approximately:

- 111 calories
- 16 grams protein

Artichoke and Egg Spread

We love artichokes and egg salad. How about putting the two of them together, adding some curry powder for rich taste, and calling it lunch over some fresh greens or on cucumber slices, in celery, or just by the spoonful? Lots of choices and good flavors make it great for breakfast or lunch or to serve as canapés.

Ingredients:

- 1 dozen hard-boiled eggs
- 1 (14 ounce) can artichoke hearts (packed in water)
- 1½ teaspoons curry powder, or to taste
- Sea salt and freshly ground pepper, to taste
- Dash of cayenne (if you desire extra heat)
- 1 cup nonfat Greek yogurt

Directions:

1. Remove yolks from half of hard-boiled eggs. Discard yolks.
2. Chop hard-boiled egg whites with remaining hard-boiled eggs. Place in mixing bowl.
3. Drain artichoke hearts and chop. Add to chopped eggs and stir.
4. Add curry powder, salt, pepper, and optional cayenne.
5. Add yogurt and mix well.
6. Cover and refrigerate for an hour or so to allow flavors to blend.
7. Serve as desired.

Nutrition: Makes 4 generous servings. Each serving has approximately:

- 200 calories
- 22 grams protein
- and a bit of an exotic taste!

Barbecue Stir-Fry

This is an easy lunch or dinner for one with several ways to substitute and meet *your* personal tastes. Let's start with the basics, and you can vary it from there. This will make a meal for one, or you could double it for two, or triple…well, you get the picture, right?

Ingredients:

- 2 cups broccoli slaw
- ¼ cup water
- 3 ounces 96 percent lean ground beef
- Granulated garlic and onion, to taste
- 2 tablespoons barbecue sauce (choose a sauce with no more than 45 calories per serving)

Directions:

1. Spray 10-inch skillet with nonstick cooking spray (a current favorite is coconut oil spray) and bring to medium-high heat.
2. Add broccoli slaw and water.
3. Cover and cook for 4–6 minutes or until fully softened.
4. Remove lid. If necessary, cook and stir until water has completely evaporated.
5. Remove slaw from pan and cover to keep warm.
6. Spray skillet with nonstick spray again and return to heat. Add beef and garlic and onion to taste (about ⅛ to ¼ teaspoon of each).
7. Cook and crumble beef for about 2–3 minutes, making sure beef is completely cooked.

8. Return broccoli slaw to skillet, add barbecue sauce, and cook and stir until thoroughly mixed and heated. Serve hot and enjoy!

Nutrition: Makes 1 serving.

- 200 calories
- 22 grams protein

Variations (be sure to adjust nutrition accordingly):

- Use ground turkey or ground chicken instead of ground beef.
- Use spaghetti squash or zoodles (zucchini spaghetti made with a Veggetti) instead of broccoli slaw.

Bikini-Ready Crab Salad

We used fresh crab, but you can also use canned crab. Eat with a fork, add to a mixed greens salad, or wrap it up in a piece of crisp romaine lettuce.

Ingredients:

- Grandma Sims Cucumber and Onion Salad (recipe below)
- 3 ounces chopped fresh crab
- 1 tablespoon low-calorie mayo with olive oil
- ¼ teaspoon seasoned salt

Directions for Bikini-Ready Crab Salad:

1. Add ⅓ cup Grandma Sims Cucumber and Onion Salad to bowl.
2. Add all other ingredients. Toss to coat and mix well.
3. Serve and enjoy!

Grandma Sims Cucumber and Onion Salad
Ingredients:

- 4 mini cucumbers, sliced thin
- ⅓ cup water
- 1 packet Splenda (or zero-calorie sweetener of your choice)
- ⅓ cup apple cider vinegar
- salt and pepper, to taste
- ½ teaspoon seasoned salt
- ½ red onion, sliced thin

Directions for Grandma Sims Cucumber and Onion Salad:

1. Mix all ingredients together and store in fridge. The longer it sits, the better it gets.

Nutrition: Makes 1 serving.

- 125 calories
- 15.9 grams protein

BW's Shrimp Po'Boy
A great way to use up leftover shrimp.

Ingredients: Shrimp Po'Boy

- 1 thin slice whole-grain toast,
- 1 teaspoon Dijon mustard
- 2 slices turkey bacon, cooked
- ⅓ cup Grandma's Cucumber and Onion Salad (see below)
  2 ounces cooked shrimp, tail removed (can be plain or seasoned with salt and pepper)

Directions: Shrimp Po'Boy

1. Add toast to plate, then spread on Dijon mustard.
2. Place turkey bacon on top of mustard, then add Grandma's Cucumber and Onion Salad.
3. Top with shrimp and enjoy!

Grandma's Cucumber and Onion Salad
Ingredients:

- 4 mini cucumbers, sliced thin
- ⅓ cup water
- 1 packet Splenda (or zero-calorie sweetener of your choice)
- ⅓ cup apple cider vinegar
- salt and pepper, to taste
- ½ teaspoon seasoned salt
- ½ red onion, sliced thin

Directions for Grandma's Cucumber and Onion Salad:

Mix all ingredients together. Keeps for four days in fridge.

Nutrition for Shrimp Po'Boy: Makes 1 serving.

- 187.4 calories
- 15.9 grams protein

Canadian Bacon Pizza in Less Than 15 Minutes

Here is a quick and simple lunch that scores nine out of ten. Just add crushed red pepper if you like it hot.

Ingredients:

- 12 slices uncured Canadian bacon.
- ½ cup Trader Joe's Traditional Marinara Sauce
- 2 ounces Trader Joe's Lite Shredded Mozzarella Cheese

Directions:

1. Preheat oven to 475 degrees.
2. Cover baking pan with foil and spray lightly with nonstick cooking spray.
3. Arrange Canadian bacon slices in threes, overlapping slightly on pan.
4. Add 2 tablespoons sauce to each grouping.
5. Add ½ ounce cheese to each grouping.
6. Bake for 6–8 minutes until cheese is melted and beginning to brown.

Nutrition: Makes 2 servings.
Each serving has approximately:

- 180 calories
- 27.5 grams protein

Chicken Burgers Mediterranean for Breakfast or Lunch

Burgers, patties—whatever you want to call them, and whenever you choose to eat them—delicious is what they are.

Ingredients:

- ½ onion, chopped
- 2 cloves garlic, chopped
- 10 ounces fresh spinach, chopped
- ½ teaspoon sea salt
- ½ teaspoon freshly ground pepper
- 1 teaspoon ground nutmeg
- 1 pound extra-lean ground chicken
- ¼ cup panko bread crumbs
- ¼ cup egg substitute
- ½ teaspoon freshly ground lemon pepper
- 1 teaspoon garlic powder
- 1 teaspoon onion powder
- 1 teaspoon oregano
- 1 tablespoon dried parsley
- Toppings: cheese, tomato slices

Directions:

1. Spray skillet with olive oil spray and preheat to medium.
2. Add onion and sauté for 3–4 minutes or until soft.
3. Add garlic. Mix and cook for another 2 minutes.
4. Add spinach. Mix and cook for 3 minutes.
5. Mix in salt, pepper, and nutmeg.
6. Remove mixture from pan and add to mixing bowl. Allow to cool (put it in the refrigerator for about 10 minutes).

7. Add ground chicken, bread crumbs, egg substitute, and remaining seasonings to mixing bowl. Mix well.
8. Form into 8 patties and chill for at least 10 minutes in refrigerator (this helps the patties stay together on the grill).
9. Grill over medium heat or in pan on stove, or broil for about 3–4 minutes per side, turning once. Internal temperature should be around 165 degrees.
10. Serve hot.

PRO-TIP: For **lunch**, top burgers with your favorite cheese (be sure to add the calories/protein) and a tomato slice. Wrap cooled leftovers and store in the refrigerator or freezer.

Use for **quick breakfasts** (microwave on 50 percent power for about 1 minute), then top with a sunny-side-up egg.

For **quick lunches**, microwave on 50 percent power for about 1 minute, then add cheese (feta crumbles would be great on this) and microwave for 10 seconds more, or heat in a skillet over medium heat until warmed throughout.

Nutrition: Makes 8 burgers.
Each burger has approximately:

*   88 calories
*   13 grams protein

Chicken Salad with Petite Peas, Celery, and Mini Sweet Peppers

Combine a couple cans of Kirkland-brand (Costco) premium chunked chicken breast, some frozen peas, chopped celery, and mini sweet peppers with some basil cream dressing to blend, and six lunch servings are ready to go! It's your choice how you serve this salad—as is, over salad greens, stuffed in a tomato, or, for the rest of the family, inside a tortilla or on toast or crackers.

Ingredients:

- 25 ounces premium chunked chicken breast (two cans of the Kirkland brand), drained
- 4 stalks celery, chopped
- 3 mini sweet peppers, chopped
- ⅔ cup frozen petite peas
- ½ cup Bolthouse Creamy Basil Dressing

Directions:

1. Mix all ingredients together in a large bowl until well blended.

Nutrition: Makes 6 servings.
Each serving has approximately:

- 125 calories
- 17.5 grams protein

Chicken Waldorf Salad

We used rotisserie chicken for this recipe, but you can use canned chicken or leftover grilled or roasted chicken and wind up with the same delicious result.

Ingredients:

- 15 ounces rotisserie chicken, chopped into bite-size pieces
- 1 small apple, chopped
- 3 stalks celery, chopped
- ¼ cup walnuts, chopped
- 15 red seedless grapes, sliced in half
- ½ tablespoon lemon pepper
- 1 cup nonfat plain Fage Greek yogurt
- 1 tablespoon honey

Directions:

1. In large mixing bowl, add chicken, apple, celery, walnuts, grapes, and lemon pepper. Stir to mix well.
2. Add yogurt and honey and mix well, making sure to "wet" all ingredients.
3. Place in individual containers and refrigerate to blend flavors.
4. Serve in individual containers. Eat with fork, over greens, wrapped in crisp lettuce leaves, on rice cakes, or in any way you choose.

Nutrition: Makes 8 servings.
Each serving has approximately:

- 142.5 calories
- 19 grams protein

Chopped Chicken Bacon Ranch Salad

Use leftover grilled chicken breast or rotisserie chicken breast to make this simple lunch in minutes.

Ingredients:

- 4 ounces cooked chicken breast, chopped
- ¼ cup shredded light Mexican cheese
- 1 romaine lettuce leaf, chopped
- 1 tablespoon real bacon bits
- 2 tablespoons Bolthouse Greek Yogurt Peppercorn Ranch Dressing

Directions:

1. Add chicken, cheese, lettuce, and bacon to your serving bowl.
2. Top with dressing and enjoy!

Nutrition: Makes 1 serving.

- 265 calories
- 43 grams protein

Crab, Peas, plus Bacon Salad
A protein and produce lunch.

Ingredients:

- ½ pound chopped crabmeat
- 8 ounces peas
- 6 ounces center-cut bacon, crumbled
- ¼ cup nonfat plain Fage Greek yogurt
- ¼ cup low-calorie mayo with olive oil
- Salt, pepper, and/or Mrs. Dash® Table Blend, to taste.

Directions:

1. Mix all ingredients together and serve.

Nutrition: Makes 4 servings.
Each ½-cup serving has approximately:

- 202.5 calories
- 17.0 grams protein

Cranberry Chicken Salad

Great to eat with fresh veggies or a fork, or add a cheese slice and broil for two minutes for a warm, tasty meal.

Ingredients:

- 16 ounces cooked chicken, chopped
- ⅓ cup celery, diced
- ¼ cup dried cranberries
- ¼ cup slivered almonds
- ¾ cup low-calorie mayo with olive oil
- 6 ounces nonfat plain Fage Greek yogurt
- 1 tablespoon lemon juice

Directions:

1. Place all ingredients into medium-sized mixing bowl.
2. Mix with fork to combine.
3. Serve and enjoy.

Nutrition: Makes 5 servings.
Each ½-cup serving has:

- 235 calories
- 23 grams protein

Curried Rotisserie Chicken Salad with Apples, Craisins, and Celery

Costco's rotisserie chicken is great because the meat is always tender, and you can strip it off the bones, toss the bones and skin, and freeze it to use at a later time. We used a 15-ounce package to make this company-worthy delicious curried chicken salad.

Ingredients:

- 15 ounces rotisserie chicken, boned, skinned, and chopped
- 4 stalks celery, chopped
- 1 small apple, chopped
- ¼ cup craisins
- 6 tablespoons Bolthouse Cilantro Avocado Yogurt Dressing
- 1 tablespoon curry powder

Directions:

1. Mix all ingredients together and chill.
2. Place into eight individual containers and refrigerate.

Nutrition: Makes 8 servings.
Each serving has approximately:

- 129 calories
- 16 grams protein

Fajita Chicken Salad

Fill lettuce cups with this salad, eat it with a fork, or enjoy it on a slice of whole-grain toast.

Ingredients:

- ½ cup low-calorie mayo with olive oil
- 1 tablespoon fajita seasoning
- 3 cups cooked chicken breast, chopped
- ¼ cup yellow onion, diced
- ½ medium red bell pepper, diced
- ½ medium yellow pepper, diced
- ¼ cup cilantro, chopped

Directions:

1. Add mayo and fajita seasoning to small mixing bowl and mix well.
2. Add all remaining ingredients to medium-sized bowl.
3. Add mayo mixture to bowl with chicken and mix until all ingredients are well coated.

Nutrition: Makes 6 servings.
Each ½-cup serving has:

- 146.3 calories
- 21.1 grams protein

Ham and Swiss—No Rye Bread, Please

Quick and easy lunch that can be thrown into containers and assembled just about anywhere.

Ingredients:

- 2 ounces black forest ham (buy a double package from Costco, divide it into small bags, and freeze it)
- 2 slices Jarlsberg light swiss cheese
- 2 teaspoons mustard

Directions:

1. If using larger package, weigh out 2 ounces of ham.
2. Cut swiss cheese to fit ham slices and place on top.
3. Add dollop of mustard, roll up, and enjoy.

Nutrition: Makes one serving.

- 130 calories
- 17 grams protein

Holy Bowl of Yum
A great way to use up leftover Muscle Burgers.

Main Ingredients:

- ½ cup nonfat refried beans, cooked
- ⅓ cup Shallots and Sweet Pepper Salad (see recipe below)
- 1 Muscle Burger, reheated and chopped (recipe on page #122)
- 1 tablespoon vinaigrette (see recipe below)

Directions for Holy Bowl of Yum:

1. Add beans and shallot and pepper salad to bowl
2. Add chopped burger pieces.
3. Pour vinaigrette over other ingredients and toss.

Shallots and Sweet Pepper Salad

- 1 shallot, sliced thin
- ⅓ cup water
- 1 packet Splenda
- ⅓ cup apple cider vinegar
- Salt and pepper, to taste
- ½ teaspoon seasoned salt
- 2 cups thinly sliced mini sweet peppers

Directions:

1. Mix all ingredients together. Can be stored for up to three days in fridge.

Vinaigrette

- ¼ cup extra-virgin olive oil
- 2 tablespoons red wine vinegar
- Juice of 1 lemon
- 1 teaspoon dried oregano
- Salt and pepper, to taste

Directions:

1. Pour into measuring cup and whisk until smooth. Can be stored for up to seven days in fridge.

Nutrition for Holy Bowl of Yum: Makes 1 serving.

- 323.8 calories
- 32.3 grams protein

Italian Style Chopped Salad

This takes about seven or eight minutes to toss together and is worth the effort. So many more goodies could be added, and they would certainly change the nutrition, so don't forget to add up the extra calories when you make additions.

Ingredients:

- 1 cup power greens, roughly chopped (baby spinach, baby kale, and baby swiss chard)
- 1 mini sweet pepper, chopped
- 1 ounce jicama root, chopped
- 1 ounce fresh mozzarella cheese, chopped
- 1 slice reduced-fat provolone cheese, chopped
- 6 slices Gallo Light Dry Italian Salame, chopped
- 3 slices turkey breast, chopped (The brand used had 45 calories/10 grams protein for the three slices)
- Dash of dried basil (or 1 or 2 leaves fresh basil, chopped)
- 1 tablespoon balsamic vinegar

Directions:

1. Toss all ingredients together in a bowl and dig in!

Nutrition: Makes 1 serving.

- 268 calories
- 29.7 grams protein

Kitchen Sink Tuna Salad

Every now and then tossing a little bit of almost everything in the refrigerator into a bowl results in a winner.

Ingredients:

- 3 (5.51 ounce) cans albacore tuna in water
- 6 hard-boiled egg whites
- 4 mini sweet peppers, chopped
- 4 stalks celery, chopped
- 3 tablespoons bacon bits
- 10 tablespoons Bolthouse Creamy Basil Dressing
- 3 tablespoons Trader Joe's Olive Tapenade
- 2 teaspoons Trader Joe's Aioli Garlic Mustard Sauce

Directions:

1. In large bowl, mix together tuna, egg whites, peppers, celery, and bacon bits until evenly distributed.
2. Add wet ingredients and mix thoroughly.
3. Refrigerate for at least 30 minutes to let flavors blend, or portion into small containers and refrigerate for use throughout the week.

Nutrition: Makes 8 servings.
Each ¾-cup serving has approximately:

- 133 calories
- 21 grams protein

Lunch Done Right
Super quick and delicious!

Ingredients: Lunch Done Right

- 1 teaspoon Dijon mustard
- 1 thin slice whole-grain toast
- ½ serving No-Mayo Hummus Tuna Salad (see recipe below)
- ⅓ cup thinly sliced cucumbers
- Salt and pepper, to taste

Directions: Lunch Done Right

1. Spread mustard on toast.
2. Add No-Mayo Hummus Tuna Salad to toast.
3. Next, add cucumber slices. Sprinkle with salt and pepper as desired.

No-Mayo Hummus Tuna Salad

- 1 (5 ounce) can yellowfin tuna in oil
- 1 tablespoon Sabra roasted garlic hummus
- 1 tablespoon Dijon mustard
- ¼ teaspoon garlic salt
- ¼ teaspoon Lawry's seasoned salt
- ¼ teaspoon pepper
- ⅓ cup diced red onion

Directions:

1. Mix all ingredients together and divide into two servings.
2. One serving is needed for Lunch Done Right.

Nutrition for Lunch Done Right: Makes 1 serving.

- 192.5 calories
- 16.9 grams protein

Oh My Heaven Creamy Salmon Salad

Eat with cucumbers, lettuce leaves, or even a serving of Triscuits crackers.

Ingredients:

- 1 (6 ounce) can Alaskan salmon
- 1 tablespoon low-calorie mayo with olive oil
- 1 tablespoon lemon juice
- 1 teaspoon dill weed, chopped
- ½ cup chopped red onion
- 3 ounces Greek cream cheese
- 1 tablespoon dill pickle relish
- Salt and pepper, to taste

Directions:

1. Place all ingredients in medium-sized mixing bowl.
2. Use fork to mix all ingredients together well.

Nutrition: Makes 3 servings.
Each ½-cup serving has:

- 156 calories
- 17.4 grams protein

Olives, Eggs, and Cottage Cheese—Oh My!

Combine hard-boiled eggs or hard-boiled egg whites (toss out the yolks), cottage cheese, and a jar of Trader Joe's Green Olive Tapenade, and your breakfast or lunch plate will be happy.

Ingredients:

- 2 hard-boiled egg whites (toss out the yolks to save some calories and add more protein)
- ½ cup cottage cheese (low fat)
- 2 tablespoons Trader Joe's Green Olive Tapenade

Directions:

1. Mash hard-boiled egg whites in bowl with fork.
2. Add cottage cheese and tapenade. Mix well and enjoy!

Nutrition: Makes 1 serving.

- 166 calories
- 19.6 grams protein

Pop of Color Lunch Bowl
A great way to use up leftover burgers.

Ingredients: Main Recipe

- ½ medium sweet potato, cooked and mashed
- ⅓ cup Grandma's Cucumber and Onion Salad (see recipe below)
- 4 ounces cooked lean ground sirloin burger, chopped and reheated
- 1 tablespoon Best-Ever Dressing (see recipe below)

Directions for Pop of Color Lunch Bowl:

1. Add sweet potato, cucumber and onion salad
2. Add chopped burger to bowl.
3. Pour Best-Ever Dressing over bowl and toss all ingredients together.

Grandma's Cucumber and Onion Salad

- 4 seedless cucumbers, sliced thin
- ⅓ cup water
- 1 packet Splenda
- ⅓ cup apple cider vinegar
- Salt and pepper, to taste
- ½ teaspoon seasoned salt
- ½ red onion, sliced thin

Directions:

1. Mix all ingredients together. Keeps for four days in fridge.

Best-Ever Dressing

- ½ cup extra-virgin olive oil
- ¼ cup apple cider vinegar
- 1 tablespoon garlic, minced
- 1 teaspoon honey
- 1 teaspoon Dijon mustard
- Salt and pepper, to taste

Directions:

1. Pour into a measuring cup and whisk. Keeps for seven days in fridge.

Nutrition for Pop of Color Lunch Bowl: Makes 1 serving.

- 288.4 calories
- 26.92 grams protein

Some Like It Greek Chicken Salad

It's amazing how a few ingredients can be mixed together for a quick and tasty chicken salad.

Ingredients:

- 2 (12.5 ounce) cans chicken breast
- 4 stalks celery, chopped
- 4 tablespoons chopped olives
- 2 ounces feta cheese, crumbled
- 5 tablespoons Bolthouse Creamy Roasted Garlic Dressing

Directions:

1. Drain cans of chicken in colander. Lightly rinse chicken with cold water to remove excess salt.
2. In large bowl, add chicken, celery, olives, and feta cheese.
3. Stir well to mix.
4. Add garlic dressing and mix well again.
5. Serve immediately, or portion and refrigerate for later use.

Nutrition: Makes 6 servings.
Each serving has approximately:

- 122 calories
- 17.5 grams protein

Southwestern Turkey Salad

This recipe was made from the leftovers of a whole cooked turkey. It is quick easy and delicious. Eat it with a fork, in a wrap, on a sandwich, or on a bed of greens.

Ingredients:

- 13 ounces cooked turkey, chopped
- 3 mini sweet peppers, chopped
- 4 stalks celery, chopped
- 2 tablespoons Hatch green chile salsa
- 1 cup chopped power greens
- ½ cup Bolthouse Cilantro Avocado Dressing

Directions:

1. Measure and mix all ingredients in large bowl.
2. Put the measured portions in individual containers for quick grab-and-go meals.

Nutrition: Makes 8 servings.
Each serving has approximately:

- 92.5 calories
- 15.5 grams protein

Strawberry Fields Forever Salad

When strawberries are in season and they are at their biggest and juiciest, add them to lots things for that sweet flavor.

Ingredients:

- 1 cup baby spinach
- ¼ cucumber, chopped
- 1 ounce jicama root, chopped
- 2.5 ounces deli turkey meat, cut into bite-size pieces
- 1 ounce feta cheese, crumbled
- 3 large strawberries, sliced thin
- 2 tablespoons Opa Tzatziki Ranch Greek Yogurt Dressing

Directions:

1. In bowl, layer baby spinach, cucumber, jicama, turkey, feta crumbles, and sliced strawberries.
2. Top with salad dressing and enjoy.

Nutrition: Makes 1 serving.

- 239 calories
- 23 grams protein

Summer Chicken Salad

This is great to eat with fresh veggies, on a half slice of toasted multigrain bread, or simply with a fork.

Ingredients:

- 16 ounces chicken breast, chopped
- ¼ cup slivered almonds
- 6 ounces nonfat plain Fage Greek yogurt
- ¼ cup low-calorie mayo with olive oil
- ¼ cup basil, chopped
- 1 (11 ounce) can mandarin oranges, strained
- 1 tablespoon juice, reserved from mandarin oranges

Directions:

1. Place all ingredients into medium-sized mixing bowl.
2. Mix with fork to combine, coating chicken with other ingredients.
3. Serve and enjoy.

Nutrition: Makes 5 servings.
Each ½-cup serving has:

- 281 calories
- 27 grams protein

Sun-Dried Tomato and Basil Pesto Yellowfin Tuna Salad

Great to eat with fresh veggies, stuffed in pita bread, or simply with a fork.

Ingredients:

- 2 (5 ounce) cans yellowfin tuna in oil
- ¼ cup basil pesto
- ¼ cup sun-dried tomatoes
- 6 ounces plain nonfat Greek yogurt
- Salt and pepper, to taste

Directions:

1. Place all ingredients in medium-sized mixing bowl.
2. Mix with fork to combine.
3. Serve and enjoy.

Nutrition: Makes 4 servings.
Each ½-cup serving has:

- 242.5 calories
- 20 grams protein

Tuna and Egg Salad Dressed Up

Mom used to mix tuna, hard-boiled eggs, and mayonnaise for our tuna salad sandwiches. Sometimes she would add a little celery. This dressed-up version has fewer calories, lots of flavor, and works without the bread.

Ingredients:

- 3 (6 ounce) cans Kirkland albacore tuna, packed in water
- 1 hard-boiled egg
- 3 hard-boiled egg whites
- 4 medium-sized stalks celery, chopped
- 4 mini sweet peppers, chopped
- ½ cup Bolthouse Creamy Basil Dressing

Directions:

1. Open and drain tuna (lightly rinse it) and place in large bowl.
2. Add hard-boiled egg to tuna, then add hard-boiled egg whites. (If you have a dog, Fido would probably love it if you added the leftover egg yolks to his or her dinner.)
3. With large fork, mash eggs and mix thoroughly with tuna, breaking tuna into chunks.
4. Add celery and peppers to tuna mixture and blend thoroughly.
5. Add salad dressing and mix thoroughly so all dry ingredients are "wet" with dressing.
6. Measure out your portions and enjoy!

Nutrition: Makes 8 servings.
Each serving has approximately:

- 127 calories
- 21.5 grams protein

<u>PRO-TIP</u>: Store this salad in individual containers in the re-frigerator for the week. It can be eaten out of the container, on top of salad greens, scooped with mini pepper chunks, stuffed into a tomato, wrapped in a big lettuce leaf, or in any way your imagination allows.

Turkey Salad with Olives, Celery, and Feta Dill Dressing

Here's another quick and easy way to use leftover turkey. It would also work well with chicken.

Ingredients:

- 7 ounces roast turkey, chopped
- 8 large black olives, chopped
- 2 stalks celery, chopped
- 4 tablespoons Opa Feta Dill Greek Yogurt Dressing

Directions:

1. Mix all ingredients together in large bowl.
2. Portion and serve.

Nutrition: Makes 3 servings.
Each serving has approximately:

- 152 calories
- 19 grams protein

Wicked Good Chicken Salad

Great to eat with fresh veggies, on half of a toasted English muffin, or simply with a fork.

Ingredients:

- 3 cups cooked chicken, chopped
- 2 green onions, sliced thin
- 2 ounces roasted red peppers
- 1 small carrot, grated
- 1 stalk celery, diced
- ¼ cup diced red onion
- ⅔ cup nonfat plain Fage Greek yogurt
- ¼ cup parsley, chopped
- 2 tablespoons chives, chopped
- 1 tablespoon dill weed, chopped
- 1 tablespoon minced garlic
- ¼ teaspoon garlic powder
- ½ teaspoon onion powder
- ¼ cup low-fat buttermilk
- Salt and pepper, to taste

Directions:

1. Place all ingredients in medium-sized mixing bowl.
2. Using fork, mix to combine, coating chicken and veggies with rest of ingredients.
3. Serve and enjoy.

Nutrition: Makes 6 servings.
Each ½-cup serving has:

- 198 calories
- 25.3 grams protein

Dinners

A LONG WITH BEING family friendly, your dinners need to be tasty treasures that are protein and produce packed. Leftovers from this section make great lunches, or you can freeze them for additional dinners later in the week or month.

Asian Beef with Snow Peas

A quick stir-fry is great for dinner, and this fits the bill completely. Quick, easy, protein packed, and delicious. Eating with chopsticks will slow you down.

Ingredients:

- 3 tablespoons soy sauce
- 2 tablespoons rice wine
- 1 tablespoon brown sugar
- ½ teaspoon cornstarch
- 1 tablespoon fresh ginger, minced
- 1 tablespoon minced garlic
- 1 pound beef round steak, cut into thin strips
- 8 ounces snow peas

Directions:

1. Combine soy sauce, rice wine, brown sugar, and cornstarch in a small bowl. Set aside.
2. Spray skillet or wok with nonstick cooking spray and set over medium heat.
3. Stir-fry ginger and garlic for 30 seconds.
4. Add steak pieces and stir-fry for about 2 minutes until evenly browned.
5. Add snow peas and stir-fry for another 3 minutes.
6. Add soy sauce mixture and bring to a boil, stirring constantly.
7. Lower heat and simmer until sauce thickens, about 1 minute.
8. Serve immediately.

Nutrition: Makes 4 servings.
Each serving has approximately:

- 275 calories
- 38 grams protein

Avocado Chicken Burgers

Ground chicken, avocado, and some onion make for a burger that is delish. Grill them, broil them, or cook them in a pan on the stove—whatever works best for you at the moment.

Ingredients:

- 1 pound ground chicken
- 6 tablespoons finely chopped sweet onion
- ½ teaspoon sea salt
- ½ teaspoon freshly ground pepper
- 4 tablespoons mashed avocado
- Cheese slices, optional

Directions:

1. Preheat outdoor grill to medium heat or prepare your broiling pan or frying pan with nonstick cooking spray.
2. In bowl, combine chicken, onion, salt, and pepper, mixing well (you can use your hands).
3. Divide into four equal portions, rolling each into a ball.
4. One by one, take each chicken ball and flatten on plate to be about ¼- to ½-inch thick.
5. Add 1 tablespoon of mashed avocado to each flattened burger and then fold sides into each other, sealing in avocado and making patties. Repeat until all four are done; refrigerate for at least half an hour to help burgers hold together on grill.
6. Grill for about 4 minutes per side or until internal temperature is 165 degrees.
7. Add cheese if desired and serve hot.

<u>PRO-TIP</u>: These can be wrapped in lettuce, served with a slice of cheese and/or a slice of tomato on top, or in a bun for the rest of the family.

Nutrition: Makes 4 servings.
Each serving has approximately:

- 172 calories
- 21 grams protein

Bacon Bleu Cheese Burgers

Every now and then a burger fresh off the grill sounds great. Make it full flavored so each bite is a tasty treat. These burgers do just that.

Ingredients:

- 8 ounces 96 percent lean ground beef
- Salt, pepper, and granulated garlic, to taste
- 1 ounce bleu cheese, cut into two pieces
- 4 slices center-cut bacon
- Toothpicks

Directions:

1. Using your hands, mix ground beef and salt, pepper, and granulated garlic.
2. Divide beef mixture in half.
3. Flatten out each half and place cheese slice in center of each.
4. Roll up edges around cheese and seal patty shut.
5. Wrap two bacon slices around each rolled-up burger, securing with toothpicks as necessary.
6. Grill, turning frequently until bacon and beef are cooked to your liking.
7. Move to plate, remove toothpicks, and enjoy!

Nutrition: Makes 2 burgers.
Each burger has approximately:

- 230 calories
- 28 grams protein

Baked Mozzarella Chicken Rolls

This takes some prep time, but it will be worth it. All of the flavors, textures, and cheesy goodness will please both you *and* your family. We counted *all* of the calories/protein in the egg and the bread crumbs but doubt you will use it all when you make the recipe.

Ingredients:

- 2 pounds boneless, skinless chicken breasts
- 1 cup panko bread crumbs
- 6 tablespoons grated Parmesan cheese, divided
- 5 ounces fresh baby spinach, chopped
- 1 clove garlic, minced
- ½ cup part-skim ricotta cheese
- ⅓ cup egg whites or egg substitute
- 1 cup marinara sauce (we use a pasta sauce from Trader Joe's at 45 calories per ½ cup)
- 3 ounces thinly sliced fresh mozzarella cheese
- Fresh basil, to garnish

Directions:

1. Cut chicken into 8 (4-ounce) pieces and pound until thin (to allow for quick cooking and more filling).
2. Place bread crumbs in shallow bowl with 2 tablespoons Parmesan cheese. Mix with a fork and set aside.
3. Spray pan with olive oil spray and sauté spinach and garlic until spinach is just barely wilted (2–3 minutes).
4. Combine sautéed spinach with ricotta, remaining Parmesan, and 2–3 tablespoons egg whites.

5. Place remaining egg whites in shallow bowl and set aside.
6. Preheat oven to 450 degrees. Prepare large baking dish with nonstick cooking spray.
7. Place one piece of chicken on flat work surface. Put spoonful of ricotta-spinach filling right in middle and roll chicken up so that its edges meet to form a seam.
8. Dip entire chicken roll into egg whites and then roll it in bread crumbs.
9. Place in prepared baking dish seam-side down.
10. Repeat process with remaining chicken pieces.
11. Bake for 25 minutes or until chicken is cooked through.
12. Remove from oven. Cover chicken with marinara sauce and mozzarella slices.
13. Bake for another 3–5 minutes or until cheese is melted.
14. Sprinkle with basil and serve hot.

Nutrition: Makes 8 servings.
Each serving has approximately:

- 259 calories
- 35.1 grams protein

Baked Shrimp Parm
Italian night done right!

Ingredients:

- 1 pound shrimp, peeled, deveined, and tails removed
- Salt and freshly ground pepper, to taste
- 1½ cups Rustico Sauce from Traders Joe's (or any low-sugar marinara sauce)
- 2 cups shredded light mozzarella cheese
- 2 tablespoons Parmesan cheese
- 20 shakes Johnny's Garlic Spread and Seasoning (or any comparable garlic seasoning)
- Extra-virgin olive oil spray

Directions:

1. Preheat oven to 400 degrees.
2. Line baking sheet with parchment paper and spray with nonstick cooking spray.
3. Place shrimp individually on paper.
4. Give each shrimp a crank of freshly ground pepper and a dash of salt.
5. Add 1 tablespoon marinara sauce to each shrimp.
6. Add 1 tablespoon mozzarella to each shrimp.
7. Divide and distribute Parmesan cheese onto shrimp. (use your fingers—just a little bit on each shrimp.)
8. Give each shrimp a shake of garlic seasoning.
9. Spray shrimp with olive oil spray.

10. Bake for 16 minutes, then broil on high for 2 minutes; watch shrimp carefully. When cheese starts to brown, the shrimp is done.
11. Serve as a standalone meal or pair with pasta, zoodles, cauliflower rice, or salad.

Nutrition: Makes 4 servings.
Each serving (5 shrimp) has:

- 215.5 calories
- 27.5 grams protein

Basil Pesto Italian Sausage and Cauliflower Casserole

Serve this delicious meal to your family with salad and garlic bread. It makes for great leftovers to take for lunches at work or for busy weeknights when you just want to grab, heat, and eat.

Ingredients:

- 1 (20 ounce) bag frozen cauliflower rice
- 2 tablespoons Brummel & Brown Spread
- ¼ cup nonfat milk
- 1 pound ground chicken Italian sausage (you can use chicken sausage in link casings; just remove from the casing and crumble)
- Salt and pepper, to taste
- 1 tablespoon garlic powder
- ½ cup shredded mozzarella cheese, divided
- ¼ cup Parmesan cheese
- 5 tablespoons basil pesto, divided
- ½ cup pizza sauce, divided
- 4 slices provolone cheese

Directions:

1. Preheat oven to 375 degrees. Coat 11 x 7-inch baking dish with nonstick cooking spray.
2. Combine cauliflower rice in microwave-safe bowl with yogurt butter and milk. Stir to coat cauliflower rice and then microwave for 6 minutes or more, until soft.
3. Heat large skillet over medium heat and cook sausage until done. Remove from heat.

4. Place cooked cauliflower rice in bowl of stand mixer or blender and process until smooth.
5. Add a generous amount of salt and pepper, garlic powder, ¼ cup of mozzarella, Parmesan, and 3 tablespoons basil pesto to cauliflower. Blend until smooth.
6. Spread half of cauliflower mixture over bottom of prepared baking dish.
7. Spread ¼ cup of pizza sauce on top of cauliflower mixture.
8. Scatter 2 tablespoons basil pesto on top of pizza sauce.
9. Top with half of cooked sausage and then add remaining mozzarella cheese.
10. Repeat layers (cauliflower mix, pizza sauce, cooked sausage).
11. Top with provolone.
12. Bake for 28 minutes or until cheese is melted and turning golden brown. Allow to cool a bit before serving.

Nutrition: Makes 6 servings.
Each serving has:

- 286 calories
- 28 grams protein

Basil Pesto Meatballs

These are great to eat as is, but you can cover them with marinara sauce and cheese, make them into mini sliders for the family, or chop them up and eat them in a salad.

Ingredients:

- 1 pound ground lean sirloin (use 93/7 percent lean sirloin)
- 2 eggs
- ¼ cup basil pesto sauce
- 1 tablespoon minced garlic
- 1 teaspoon lemon juice
- 1 teaspoon sea salt
- 1 teaspoon black pepper

Directions:

1. Preheat oven to 400 degrees and line baking sheet with parchment paper.
2. In large mixing bowl, combine ground sirloin and eggs.
3. Add in remaining ingredients and mix until well combined (use your hands or a stand mixer).
4. Using a tablespoon, measure out 20 meatballs.
5. Add meatballs to lined baking sheet.
6. Bake for 24 minutes.
7. Remove from oven and use spatula to remove excess fat and baked egg from meatballs.
8. Eat as is, or add marinara sauce and cheese. For the kids, add spaghetti, or you can chop them up and eat them in a salad.

Nutrition: Makes 5 servings.
Each serving (4 meatballs) has:

- 233.6 calories
- 22 grams protein

Beef and Broccoli Stir-Fry

Who needs to call for Chinese takeout when there are only one or two of you in the house and you can make it pretty simply at home—*and* have it be tasty and healthy with leftovers? Not you, that's who! You can serve this dish over some cauliflower rice.

Ingredients:

- ¾ cup beef broth
- 1 tablespoon packed light brown sugar (or you could use the Splenda mix)
- 1 tablespoon cornstarch
- 1 tablespoon soy sauce
- 1 teaspoon garlic powder
- ¼ teaspoon ground ginger
- ½ teaspoon black pepper
- Coconut oil cooking spray
- 1 pound beef round steak trimmed of all fat, cut into ¼-inch julienne strips
- 2 medium onions, cut into ½-inch wedges
- 4 cups broccoli, cut into florets

Directions:

1. In small bowl, combine broth, brown sugar, cornstarch, soy sauce, garlic powder, ginger, and pepper. Mix well, then set aside.
2. Spray wok or large skillet with coconut oil cooking spray. Set over medium-high heat and brown beef strips for about 5 minutes, stirring frequently.

3. Add onions and broccoli. Keep stirring and cook for another 3–5 minutes or until onion is tender.
4. Add beef broth mixture and stir constantly for 2–3 minutes until sauce begins to thicken. Serve immediately.

<u>PRO-TIP</u>: Add some grated orange zest for color, freshness, and a bit of zing to the taste. For those who like it spicy, Szechuan peppers can be added while stir-frying.

Nutritional info: Makes 6 servings.
Each serving has approximately:

- 190 calories
- 26 grams protein

Black Bean and Turkey Chili

What better way to have a nice hearty meal tonight—with plenty of leftovers to freeze in individual servings—than to cook a big pot of chili?

Ingredients:

- 25 ounces lean ground turkey
- 5 cups chopped onion (2 medium/large onions)
- 2 cloves garlic, chopped
- 2¼ cups chopped celery
- 2¼ cups chopped carrots
- 6 mini sweet peppers, chopped
- 3 (14.5 ounce) cans stewed tomatoes
- 2 (15.25 ounce) cans black beans, rinsed
- 1 tablespoon cumin
- 2 tablespoons chili powder
- Cayenne pepper (to taste)

Directions:

1. Sauté turkey. Drain excess juices and place in large soup pot.
2. Sauté onion, garlic, celery, carrots, and peppers just until onions are soft. Add to soup pot.
3. Add all other ingredients to pot and stir well.
4. Bring to a low boil and then reduce heat and simmer, covered, for about two hours.
5. Check seasoning levels. Add more if desired and continue simmering until chili is served.

Optional toppings: shredded cheese, nonfat plain Greek yogurt, and chopped cilantro. Don't forget to add these to your nutrition totals.

Nutrition: Makes 10 servings and has lots of healthy fiber. Each serving, without toppings, has approximately:

- 280 calories
- 22 grams protein

Bremerton Chicken Bog

A hearty meal that will make everyone happy. You can serve it with a side salad or rice for those who need a bit more with their meal.

Ingredients:

- 1 medium white onion, sliced thin
- 32 ounces low-sodium chicken broth
- 1 packet Lipton onion soup mix
- 2 teaspoons seasoned salt
- 1 teaspoon Trader Joe's 21 Seasoning Salute or Mrs. Dash® Table Blend
- 3 bay leaves
- 2 cups rotisserie chicken, skin and bones removed, chopped
- 14 ounces turkey kielbasa, sliced thin
- 1 pound cauliflower rice, cooked per package instructions
- Optional: hot sauce or crushed red pepper

Directions:

1. Spray large stockpot with nonstick cooking spray. Add onions and sauté.
2. Add broth, Lipton packet, seasoned salt, 21 Seasoning Salute, and bay leaves to stockpot and bring to a rapid boil.
3. Add chicken and kielbasa; return to rapid boil.
4. Reduce heat to medium. Cover and simmer for 20 minutes. Stir often.
5. Remove bay leaves and add cauliflower rice. Leave uncovered and simmer on medium heat for 10 minutes.

6. Serve with hot sauce or crushed red pepper for additional kick!

Nutrition: Makes 11 servings.
Each ½-cup serving has:

- 137 calories
- 14 grams protein

BW's Crock-Pot Beef & Bacon Beans

Set this one and forget it. Come home on a busy day to the smell of deliciousness filling your home.

Ingredients:

- 1 pound sliced bacon, cut into pieces
- 1 medium onion, chopped
- 1 pound 96 percent lean ground sirloin
- 1 (15 ounce) can pork and beans
- 1 (15 ounce) can kidney beans, drained and rinsed
- ½ (7.5 ounces) can great northern beans, drained and rinsed
- 1 cup ketchup
- ⅓ cup packed brown sugar
- 3 tablespoons vinegar

Directions:

1. In large skillet, cook bacon pieces. Sift and strain when cooked and place in Crock-Pot.
2. Sauté onion in same skillet until tender; remove onion with slotted spoon. Add onion on top of bacon in Crock-Pot.
3. In same skillet, cook sirloin until no longer pink, drain. Transfer sirloin to Crock-Pot.
4. Add remaining ingredients and mix well.
5. Cover and cook on low for 4 to 6 hours or until heated through.

Nutrition: Makes 12.5 servings.
Each 4-ounce serving has:

- 186 calories
- 16 grams protein

BW's Honey Walnut Shrimp

Better than Chinese takeout. You'll come back to this one often.

Ingredients:

- ½ cup water
- ¼ cup Splenda (or your choice of any powdered artificial sweetener)
- ½ cup walnuts, halved
- 1 pound shrimp, peeled, deveined, tails removed
- 3 tablespoons nonfat plain Greek yogurt
- 1 tablespoon low-calorie mayo with olive oil
- 2 tablespoons honey
- ½ teaspoon garlic powder
- ¼ teaspoon crushed red pepper
- ¼ teaspoon salt

Directions:

1. Bring water and Splenda to a boil.
2. Add walnuts and boil for 2 minutes.
3. Remove, strain, and cool walnuts.
4. Spray pan with nonstick cooking spray. Bring to medium heat. Add shrimp and cook until pink. Flip and cook another 3–4 minutes. Remove from heat.
5. While shrimp is cooking, combine other ingredients (yogurt, mayo, honey, garlic powder, crushed red pepper, and salt).
6. Add yogurt mixture and walnuts to shrimp; toss to coat.
7. Serve and smile!

Nutrition: Makes 6.5 servings.
Each 2.8-ounce serving has

- 192 calories
- 23 grams protein

Caprese Zoodles with Ground Turkey

Summertime is great for fresh tomatoes and fresh basil from the garden. Add fresh mozzarella, some ground spiced turkey, and put it over some zucchini noodles (known as *zoodles*), and it's a plate of deliciousness. You can easily substitute cooked shrimp or ground chicken or beef for the turkey.

Ingredients:

- 6 ounces extra-lean ground turkey
- 3 cloves garlic, minced
- 1 teaspoon oregano, or to taste
- ¼ teaspoon crushed red pepper, or to taste
- 20 ounces zucchini, turned into zoodles with your Veggetti or similar device
- ½ teaspoon sea salt
- ½ teaspoon freshly ground pepper
- 1 tablespoon olive oil
- 4 ounces fresh mozzarella (if ball-shaped, in half)
- 1 cup cherry tomatoes, halved
- 1 tablespoon balsamic vinegar, divided
- Fresh basil, cut into strips, for garnish

Directions:

1. Spray pan with nonstick cooking spray and heat to medium.
2. Add turkey, crumbling it as it cooks.
3. Add garlic, oregano, and crushed red pepper, and cook turkey until fully browned.
4. Remove turkey from pan and set aside.

5. Spray pan again and add zoodles, salt, and pepper, tossing and cooking just until warmed through and al dente.
6. Toss in olive oil and turkey.
7. Remove zoodle-turkey mixture from pan and place in large bowl. Add mozzarella and tomatoes, tossing to combine.
8. Serve in bowls, drizzling ¼ tablespoon balsamic vinegar and sprinkling basil over each bowl.

Nutrition: Makes 4 servings.
Each serving has approximately:

- 183 calories
- 16.8 grams protein

Chicken a La Caprese

Here's a recipe that with produce coming from all over the country and the world will let you enjoy caprese all year long, with the added protein boost of a chicken breast. Protein, produce, and great flavors mixed together. This is a dinner we would serve to "company" in a flash because it's tasty and pretty on the plate.

Ingredients:

- Sea salt and freshly ground pepper
- 4 boneless, skinless chicken breasts
- 2 teaspoons olive oil, divided
- 3 cloves garlic, minced
- 3 cups cherry tomatoes, washed and halved
- 10 large basil leaves, finely chopped
- 8 ounces fresh mozzarella, sliced about ½-inch thick
- Balsamic vinegar

Directions:

1. Salt and pepper both sides of chicken breasts.
2. Heat 1 teaspoon olive oil in large pan over medium-high heat.
3. Add chicken; cover and cook for about 10 minutes.
4. Turn chicken over and continue cooking until done.
5. While chicken is cooking, heat remaining teaspoon of olive oil in medium pan.
6. Add garlic and cook until fragrant, about 1 minute.
7. Add tomatoes and continuing sautéing until tomato skins start to soften—about 5 minutes.
8. Remove from heat. Stir in basil and set aside.

9. When chicken is done, place 2 slices of mozzarella cheese on each chicken breast.
10. Pour tomato mixture on top.
11. Cover pan to allow cheese to melt (about 1 minute).
12. Drizzle with balsamic vinegar and serve immediately.

Nutrition: Makes 4 servings.
Each serving has approximately:

- 310 calories
- 33 grams protein

Chicken Cacciatore in the Crock-Pot My Way

When looking up chicken cacciatore recipes, the common denominator is always the chicken, garlic, onions, and tomato sauce. Toss all of that into the Crock-Pot along with lots more veggies for a one-dish meal that is sure to please everyone in the family. Or at least you'll have six portions for yourself that will freeze nicely.

Ingredients:

- 1 pound boneless, skinless chicken breasts or chicken tenders
- 1 medium onion, sliced thin
- 4 cloves garlic, minced
- 7 sweet mini peppers, sliced
- 1 can (14 ounces) artichoke hearts packed in water, drained and quartered
- 2 cups quartered baby summer squash
- 1 (24 ounce) jar pasta sauce (We used Trader Joe's Organic Basil Marinara Sauce, which was 56 calories per ½ cup for this recipe)
- 1 teaspoon Italian seasoning
- ½ teaspoon dried red chili peppers (some people like it hot and spicy)
- 6 tablespoons Parmesan cheese, for garnish

Directions:

1. Starting with chicken, layer all ingredients in Crock-Pot, finishing with pasta sauce and spices.

2. Cook on low for about 6 hours or until chicken is cooked through, stirring once about halfway through to combine all the ingredients if possible (if not, stir before serving).
3. Serve, topping each serving with 1 tablespoon grated Parmesan cheese.

Nutrition: Makes 6 servings.
Each serving has approximately:

- 215 calories
- 23 grams protein

Chicken Egg Drop Soup

It takes less than fifteen minutes from start to finish to make this warm and protein-rich bowl of soup. You can add a bit of hot Chinese-style mustard to it to ensure it has some bite. Enjoy!

Ingredients:

- 1 tablespoon soy sauce
- 1 tablespoon cornstarch
- 4 cups chicken broth
- ¼ teaspoon salt
- ⅛ teaspoon white or black pepper
- 8 ounces super-firm tofu, cubed
- 1 cup sliced scallions, divided
- 3 eggs, beaten

Directions:

1. In small bowl, stir together soy sauce and cornstarch until smooth.
2. In medium pot with lid, bring broth, salt, and pepper to a boil.
3. Slowly pour in soy sauce mixture; stir and reduce heat to a low boil.
4. Stir in tofu and ½ cup scallions.
5. Simmer for 2 minutes.
6. Slowly pour beaten eggs into soup in a thin stream while stirring in a circular motion.
7. Serve immediately, garnishing bowls with remaining scallions.

Nutrition: Makes 6 servings.
Each serving has approximately:

- 150 calories
- 15 grams protein

Chicken with Mushrooms and Green Onions

Here's a quick and easy dish—it takes less than half an hour from start to finish to get it to the table—that will please many. You can serve it over or alongside some cauliflower "fried rice."

Ingredients:

- 1 tablespoon toasted sesame oil
- 1 small bunch green onions, sliced, with white and green parts separated
- 1 clove garlic, finely chopped
- 4 ounces shiitake mushrooms (caps only), sliced thin
- 4 cups water
- 2-inch piece fresh ginger, peeled and sliced into ¼-inch rounds
- ½ cup low-sodium soy sauce
- 1 pound boneless, skinless chicken breasts, cut into ¾-inch cubes

Directions:

1. In very large skillet (it will have to hold 4 cups of water plus everything else) or wok, heat sesame oil over medium heat.
2. Add white parts of green onions and garlic and cook, stirring constantly for 1 minute.
3. Add mushrooms and cook until softened, about 3 minutes more.
4. Pour water into pan and stir in ginger and soy sauce. Simmer for about 2 minutes.

5. Gently place chicken cubes into broth, reduce heat to low, cover, and poach until chicken is just cooked through—about 6–7 minutes.
6. Transfer chicken pieces to wide shallow bowls. Ladle broth over chicken.
7. Garnish with remaining green onions and serve.

Nutrition: Makes 4 servings.
Each serving has approximately:

- 190 calories
- 28 grams protein

Chinese Five-Spice Burgers

Serve these on a bun, wrap them up in lettuce leaves, or simply add them to your plate with your favorite veggies and use a fork.

Ingredients:

- 1 pound extra-lean ground turkey breast
- 2 green onions, finely chopped
- 1 teaspoon five-spice powder
- 2 tablespoons minced garlic
- 1 tablespoon ginger paste
- 3 tablespoons low-sodium soy sauce
- 5 squirts extra-virgin olive oil spray

Directions:

1. Heat oven broiler to high.
2. Line baking sheet with parchment paper.
3. Combine turkey, green onions, five-spice powder, garlic, ginger, and soy sauce in medium mixing bowl.
4. Weigh out 5 (4-ounce) meatballs.
5. Flatten each meatball into patty.
6. Place each patty on lined baking sheet and squirt with extra-virgin olive oil.
7. Place burger patties in oven and broil for 6 minutes. Remove, flip, and broil for 6 minutes more.
8. Once finished, remove and enjoy these tasty burgers.

Nutrition: Makes four servings.
Each burger has:

- 124.6 calories
- 25.21 grams protein

Cin Cin Beef and Green Beans

Amazing combination of flavors in this one. Total YUM!

Ingredients:

- 1 pound beef stew meat
- 1 (32 ounce) can crushed tomatoes
- ½ white onion, chopped
- 1 pound fresh green beans, snapped and cut into 2-inch pieces
- 1 tablespoon ground cinnamon
- 1 tablespoon sea salt
- Pepper to taste

Directions:

1. Spray Crock-Pot with nonstick cooking spray.
2. Toss meat and veggies in Crock-Pot. Sprinkle with cinnamon, salt, and pepper.
3. Stir all ingredients together until well mixed.
4. Cook on low for 8 hours.

Nutrition: Makes 9 servings.
Each 4-ounce serving has:

- 147 calories
- 11.3 grams protein

Crock-Pot Pork Salsa Verde

When the days get both shorter and colder, getting the Crock-Pot going in the morning and coming home to dinner ready to serve is our idea of how to roll. We don't think we'll hear any arguments from you guys either!

Ingredients:

- 1 large onion, cut into small wedges
- 1½ pounds boneless pork loin, cut into 1-inch pieces
- 1⅓ cups chopped tomatoes or 1 (14.5 ounces) can chopped tomatoes
- ½ cup chicken broth
- 1 (16 ounce) jar salsa verde (tomatillo salsa would work too)
- 2 cloves garlic, minced
- 1 teaspoon ground cumin
- ¼ teaspoon black pepper
- Fresh cilantro, for garnish
- Greek yogurt, for garnish

Directions:

1. Place onion and pork in Crock-Pot. Top with other ingredients.
2. Cover and cook on low for 6 hours or on high for 3 hours.
3. Serve in bowls and garnish with cilantro and 1 tablespoon of Greek yogurt.

Nutrition: Makes 6 servings.
Each 1-cup serving has approximately:

- 210 calories
- 28 grams protein

Festive Stuffed Peppers (No Rice)

Perfect for any holiday! Nobody will even notice these have no rice—the flavor is incredible. Protein and produce in every bite!

Ingredients:

- 4 bell peppers (red and green)
- 5 ounces diced onions
- 2 tablespoons minced garlic
- 1 pound lean ground sirloin
- 1 (14.5 ounces) can fire-roasted diced tomatoes
- 1 tablespoon each of cumin, paprika, onion powder, garlic powder, pepper, and Italian seasoning
- ½ cup shredded mozzarella cheese
- ½ cup cottage cheese 4% fat
- 1 tablespoon Tabasco sauce
- Dash salt

Directions:

1. Cut off tops of peppers. Bring pot of water to boil. Add peppers and boil for 3 minutes. Remove and let stand on cutting board.
2. Spray pan with nonstick cooking spray. Sauté onions and garlic until soft. Remove and add to medium-sized mixing bowl.
3. Spray pan again. Brown sirloin.
4. While the meat is browning, strain tomatoes. Reserve juice in small bowl.
5. Preheat oven to 325 degrees. Spray small baking dish with nonstick cooking spray. Add tomato juice to bottom of dish.

6. Add tomatoes, all spices, ¼ cup shredded cheese, cottage cheese, Tabasco, and mix.
7. Remove cooked meat from heat and add to tomato mixture. Mix well.
8. Place peppers in small baking dish and stuff with meat and tomato mixture.
9. Sprinkle remaining cheese on top of stuffed peppers.
10. Bake for 25 minutes, then broil on high for 2 minutes.
11. Enjoy the super festive and yummy meal!

Nutrition: Makes 4 servings.
Each serving has:

- 311 calories
- 32.4 grams protein

Fiesta Pulled Pork

Canned pulled pork? This recipe is delicious and hits the mark for vegetables, protein, fiber, and flavor. You can serve it over cauliflower rice or in tortilla shells for the family. There were lots of leftovers for dinners, lunches, and a frittata.

Ingredients:

- Olive oil cooking spray
- 1 small onion, diced
- 2 cloves garlic, minced
- 4 sweet mini peppers, diced
- 36 ounces, 3 cans Harvest Creek pulled pork in water, drained and rinsed lightly
- 1 (14.5 ounces) can stewed tomatoes
- 1 (10 ounces) can Rotel diced tomatoes with mild green chilies
- 1 (14.25 ounces) can black beans, drained
- 1 cup corn kernels
- 1 tablespoon chili powder
- 1 tablespoon cumin

Directions:

1. Spray pot with olive oil cooking spray. Add onion, garlic, and peppers. Cook over medium heat until onion is beginning to look translucent.
2. Add rest of ingredients and mix well to combine. Bring to a boil, then reduce heat. Simmer, covered, for at least an hour to blend flavors.

3. Remove cover, stir well, and continue cooking uncovered for about an hour to reduce liquid.
4. Serve and enjoy!

Nutrition: Makes 10 servings.
Each serving has approximately:

- 162 calories
- 20.5 grams protein

Get Outside of the Box Crock-Pot Chicken

Set it and forget it! Save time and feed yourself delicious food with this recipe. Serve with fresh veggies, a salad, or with your kiddos' favorite side dish.

Ingredients:

- 1 (5 pound) young chicken
- 1 large stalk celery, sliced in three pieces
- 3 green onions, sliced in 3-inch pieces
- 1 tablespoon low-sodium soy sauce
- 2 teaspoons Chinese five-spice powder

Directions:

1. Spray Crock-Pot with nonstick cooking spray and be sure to plug it in.
2. Remove giblets and innards from chicken—discard.
3. Stuff chicken with celery and onions.
4. Mix soy sauce and five-spice powder together until it makes a paste.
5. Place chicken in Crock-Pot and massage all over with soy-spice paste.
6. Cover Crock-Pot with lid and cook on low for 6–8 hours.
7. Once chicken is done cooking in Crock-Pot, turn oven broiler to high.
8. Place chicken on broiler-safe dish (if you have a rack with a dish, great. If not, anything works).
9. Place chicken under broiler for 5–8 minutes. Watch it carefully—it will crisp up quick.
10. Remove from oven and let rest for 3 minutes.

11. Remove celery and onions from inside of chicken and discard.
12. Remove skin—the nutrition stats are for *no skin eaten*—and discard.
13. Slice and serve as you like.

Nutrition: Makes 6 servings.
Each 4-ounce serving has:

- 177.16 calories
- 25.04 grams protein

Ground Beef and Pepper Skillet

Comfort food at its best. Serve over cauliflower rice or with steamed veggies.

Ingredients:

- 1 cup yellow onion, chopped
- ½ orange bell pepper, chopped
- ½ yellow bell pepper, chopped
- 2 tablespoons garlic, minced
- 1 pound 96 percent lean ground beef
- Salt and pepper, to taste
- 1 teaspoon chili powder
- 2 tablespoons fresh cilantro, chopped
- 2 green onions, chopped

Directions:

1. Prepare skillet with nonstick cooking spray. Heat skillet over medium-high heat.
2. Sauté onions, bell peppers, and garlic in skillet and cook until onions and peppers are soft, 3–4 minutes.
3. Push veggies to one edge of pan, and position that side of pan away from heat. In empty part of pan (which should be right over heat), add beef, then sprinkle with salt and chili powder.
4. Cook beef without stirring until it is browned on one side, then turn over to brown other side.
5. Once beef is cooked through, stir in onions and peppers, and sprinkle with more salt to taste. Remove from heat.

6. Stir in cilantro.
7. Serve with green onions as garnish.

Nutrition: Makes 7 servings.
Each ½-cup serving has:

- 109 calories
- 14.32 grams protein

Ground Chicken Ranch Burgers with a Bite!

Serve these on a bun, wrap them up in lettuce leaves, or simply plate with your favorite veggie and use a fork.

Ingredients:

- 1 pound ground chicken
- ¼ cup ranch seasoning
- ¼ cup diced jalapeño
- Generous amounts salt and freshly ground pepper, to taste

Directions:

1. Preheat oven broiler to high (these burgers are great on the grill or pan fried, too).
2. Line baking sheet with parchment paper or foil.
3. In medium bowl, combine chicken, ranch seasoning, diced jalapeño, salt, and pepper.
4. Divide and weigh 7 patties at 2.2 ounces each.
5. Place all 7 burgers on baking sheet.
6. Put burgers in oven with rack positioned at least 6 inches under broiler.
7. Broil 6 minutes on each side. Flip burgers after 6 minutes, then broil for another 6 minutes.

Nutrition: Makes 7 servings.
Each burger has:

- 89.2 calories
- 13 grams protein

Meat Crust Pizza

Every now and again pizza sounds wonderful. What does not sound wonderful is getting stuck on the pizza dough. Here is a meaty way to enjoy those visually appealing triangular slices (or deep dish squares). Loaded with meat and dripping with cheese, this pizza stays well within your calorie range while giving you lots of protein.

Ingredients:

- 1 pound 96 percent lean ground beef
- ½ packet dry onion soup mix
- Freshly ground pepper
- 1 egg
- 1 cup pasta sauce (should be 45 calories per ½ cup or less)
- ¼ cup grated Parmesan cheese
- 8 ounces part-skim shredded mozzarella cheese
- 17 turkey pepperoni pieces

Directions:

1. Preheat oven to 350 degrees.
2. Mix beef, soup mix, pepper, and egg in large bowl until well blended.
3. Place large piece of plastic wrap on kitchen counter.
4. Place giant meatball from mixing bowl on center of plastic wrap. Fold plastic wrap over meatball.
5. Using a rolling pin, tall glass, or wine bottle (red preferably—remember, it's pizza!), roll meat into ½-inch-thick disk.
6. Spray cookie sheet or pizza baking pan with nonstick cooking spray.

7. Carefully remove plastic wrap and place meat disk on baking pan.
8. Bake meat for 30 minutes or until cooked through.
9. Remove pan from oven and top meat crust with pasta sauce, cheese, and pepperoni.
10. Return pan to oven and bake for another 10–15 minutes or until cheese is nice and melted.
11. Remove from oven and cut into eight slices.
12. Enjoy!

PRO-TIP: You can spice this up by adding dried red peppers to it after it comes out of the oven, or you can add mushrooms, olives, bell pepper slices, or any topping of your choice before you put it in the oven. Remember to adjust the calories/protein accordingly.

Nutrition: Makes 8 servings.
Each serving has approximately:

*   200 calories
*   20 grams protein

Moroccan Shrimp with Spinach

Shrimp, spice, and spinach. Three of our favorite things. The best part? Easy cleanup since these are grilled in foil packets. In the summer, you can serve them with some thin slices of ice-cold watermelon and fresh strawberries for dessert. In the winter, you can bring this delicious dish inside by baking the foil packets in a 375-degree oven for approximately 12–15 minutes, or until shrimp is opaque and spinach is wilted.

Ingredients:

- ½ teaspoon ground coriander
- ½ teaspoon ground cumin
- ½ teaspoon paprika
- ¼ teaspoon cayenne
- Pinch ground allspice
- ¼ teaspoon sea salt, divided
- 1 pound large shrimp, peeled and deveined
- 3 tablespoons extra-virgin olive oil
- 10 ounces fresh baby spinach

Directions:

1. Mix coriander, cumin, paprika, cayenne, allspice, and ⅛ teaspoon salt in small bowl.
2. Place shrimp, oil, and remaining ⅛ teaspoon salt in large bowl. Add spice mixture, and toss to coat. Refrigerate for 30 minutes.
3. Cut four 15 x 12-inch sheets of heavy-duty foil.
4. Divide spinach and shrimp evenly among pieces of foil.
5. Bring edges of each sheet together and fold tightly to seal.

6. Preheat grill to medium-high heat. Place foil packets on grill. Close cover and cook until spinach is wilted and shrimp are opaque (5–7 minutes).
7. Serve immediately.

Nutrition: Makes 4 servings.
Each serving has approximately:

- 230 calories
- 25 grams protein

Muscle Burgers

Serve these on a bun, wrap them up in lettuce leaves, or simply plate with your favorite veggie and use a fork.

Ingredients:

- 1 pound extra-lean ground turkey breast
- 1 egg white
- ¼ cup chopped white onion
- ½ teaspoon Worcestershire sauce
- ¼ teaspoon garlic powder
- ¼ teaspoon poultry seasoning
- 2 teaspoons Dijon mustard

Directions:

1. Spray skillet with nonstick cooking spray.
2. Combine all ingredients into medium mixing bowl.
3. Weigh out 4- to 5-ounce meatballs.
4. Flatten each patty.
5. Heat skillet over medium-high heat.
6. Add burger patties to skillet and cook for 5 minutes. Flip and cook for 5 minutes more.
7. Remove and *eat for muscles*!

Nutrition: Makes 5 servings.
Each burger has:

- 104.8 calories
- 24 grams protein

Nashville Grilled Chicken

This is great to eat with fresh veggies or as a topping for a crisp mixed greens salad, or you can just enjoy it with a knife and fork.

Ingredients:

- 2 chicken breasts, sliced thin
- ¼ cup peanut oil
- 2 tablespoons 1.5 percent reduced-fat buttermilk
- 2 teaspoons Tabasco sauce
- 2 teaspoons minced garlic

Directions:

1. Combine all ingredients in large ziplock bag and store in fridge for 3 hours or overnight (the longer the better).
2. Preheat grill to medium-high heat. Place chicken breasts on hot grill. Dispose of remaining marinade. Close grill lid and let chicken cook for 6–9 minutes, only opening grill cover to flip chicken over. Cook another 6–9 minutes.
3. Cook until chicken's internal temperature is 165 degrees. Remove from grill, cover with foil, and let rest for a few minutes. Then, serve and enjoy!

Nutrition: Makes 2 servings.
Each 4-ounce serving has:

- 249 calories
- 26 grams protein

No-Mess Salmon, Asparagus, and Mango Peach Salsa

Grilling is great, cleaning the grill - not so much. Cooking with a foil packet gives you fast prep time, no oven time, *and* no cleanup time while enjoying tasty fish and veggies. If you can't grill it, pop the foil packet in the oven for 30 minutes at 400 degrees, and it will be just as good.

Ingredients:

- 20 thin asparagus spears
- Lemon pepper, to taste
- 8 ounces salmon filet
- 8 tablespoons mango peach salsa
- Dried chipotle pepper

Directions:

1. Preheat grill or oven to 400 degrees.
2. Tear off two 20 x 18-inch pieces of foil and place them crosswise over each other.
3. Wash and trim asparagus and lay out on foil.
4. Twist a few grinds of lemon pepper over asparagus.
5. Top asparagus with salmon.
6. Add a few grinds of lemon pepper and a light dusting of dried chipotle pepper to salmon.
7. Top salmon with salsa and then seal foil, making a "tent."
8. Grill for about 20 minutes (or if using oven, cook for about 30 minutes), then remove from heat.
9. Carefully cut off top of foil (hot steam will escape) and serve hot.
10. Enjoy!

Nutrition: Makes 2 servings.
Each serving has approximately:

- 240 calories
- 27.1 grams protein

Orange You Glad You Made This Delicious Bowl

Here's our take on orange chicken—but instead of chicken and rice, your bowl is filled with lean turkey, cauliflower rice, and broccoli.

Ingredients:

- 2⅔ cups cauliflower rice
- 1 tablespoon toasted sesame oil
- 1 pound extra-lean ground turkey
- 2 tablespoons minced or freshly grated ginger
- 4 cloves garlic, minced
- 1 tablespoon Asian chili-garlic sauce (or red pepper flakes could work)
- ½ cup orange juice
- 1 teaspoon orange zest
- 3 tablespoons soy sauce
- 4 cups broccoli florets
- 4 teaspoons toasted sesame seeds, to garnish

Directions:

1. In microwave-safe bowl, cover cauliflower rice loosely and microwave on high for 4 minutes. Set aside.
2. In large nonstick pan, heat sesame oil over low-medium heat. Add ground turkey and brown on all sides.
3. Add ginger, garlic, chili-garlic sauce, orange juice, orange zest, and soy sauce to pan. Stir well and bring to a simmer. Simmer on low heat for about 5 minutes, until sauce has reduced and thickened some. Stir well and remove from heat.

4. Meanwhile, in separate pot, steam broccoli in about 1 inch of water for about 4 minutes or until almost soft (or to whatever softness or crunchiness you prefer).

5. Drain broccoli. Put turkey and spice mixture back on low heat, add broccoli and cauliflower rice, and mix well to combine all flavors. When it is warmed through, serve in bowls and top each bowl with 1 teaspoon toasted sesame seeds.

Nutrition: Makes 4 servings.
Each serving has approximately:

- 237 calories
- 33 grams protein

Orgasmic Chicken BLT

Who knew that a chicken breast could be the best-tasting bun ever? This is one recipe you'll come back to over and over.

Ingredients:

- 4 ounces cooked chicken breast (can be grilled)
- ½ teaspoon Dijon mustard
- ½ teaspoon low-calorie mayo with olive oil
- 2 slices cooked center-cut bacon
- 3 thin slices of tomato, seasoned with freshly ground pepper and salt, to taste
- 1 leaf romaine lettuce

Directions:

1. Place cooked chicken breast flat on cutting board. Slice through side of breast to butterfly it. Be sure not to slice all the way through.
2. Spread mustard and mayo on inside of chicken breast.
3. Add bacon, tomato, and lettuce.
4. Grab a napkin, pick that baby up, and bite!

Nutrition: Makes 1 serving.
Each serving has:

- 198.5 calories
- 32 grams protein

Phat Greek Burgers

Serve these with Greek yogurt, cucumber slices, and pickled beets. Dress them up on a bun or just a plate for one.

Ingredients:

- 1 pound ground turkey
- 5 ounces diced red onion
- 2 ounces frozen spinach, thawed (squeeze out excess water with a paper towel)
- 1 teaspoon dried oregano
- 5 tablespoons reduced-fat feta cheese crumbles
- 1 tablespoon minced garlic
- ½ cup panko bread crumbs
- ¼ cup egg substitute
- 2 tablespoons Greek cream cheese

Directions:

1. Preheat oven broiler to high.
2. Line baking sheet with parchment paper.
3. In large bowl, combine turkey, onion, spinach, oregano, feta, garlic, panko and liquid egg. Mix well by hand or with stand mixer.
4. Divide mixture and form 6 burger patties.
5. Place all 6 burgers on baking sheet.
6. Place burgers under broiler—at least 6 inches from broiler.
7. Broil 6 minutes on each side.

Nutrition: Makes 6 servings.
Each serving has:

- 129.7 calories
- 15.3 grams protein

Pizza, Pizza! Ground Chicken Crust

Our family requests this one weekly. Best pizza crust ever and totally guilt-free.

Ingredients: Crust

- 1 pound ground chicken
- ⅓ cup Parmesan cheese
- ⅓ cup Trader Joe's low-fat mozzarella cheese
- 1 tablespoon Johnny's Garlic Spread and Seasoning
- 2 teaspoons Italian seasoning
- 2 teaspoons red bell pepper and roasted garlic seasoning
- Generous amount of freshly ground pepper

Directions: Crust

1. Preheat oven to 400 degrees.
2. Mix all ingredients together. (Use a stand mixer. If you mix by hand, remember to wash up first.)
3. Place parchment paper on pizza pan. Spray paper with non-stick cooking spray.
4. Dump chicken mixture onto paper. Wearing disposable gloves, press chicken mixture down into pan to form crust.
5. Bake 20 minutes.
6. Remove pan from oven, remove parchment paper from pan, and let cool on the counter for at least 10 minutes. Leave oven on.

Once the crust is cool, it's time to build your favorite pizza with your choice of toppings.

Ingredients: Our favorite toppings

- ½ cup pizza sauce
- 1 cup low-fat mozzarella cheese
- 1 ounce salami
- 9 slices pepperoni
- ¼ cup Parmesan cheese
- 24 pepper rings
- 1 tablespoon garlic
- 1 hefty shake of Johnny's Garlic Spread and Seasoning

1. Place parchment paper with crust back on pizza pan. Add pizza sauce and your choice of toppings.
2. Place pizza back in the oven. Bake for 10 minutes.
3. Turn oven broiler to high. Broil pizza for 4 minutes. Watch pizza carefully; when toppings start to bubble rapidly, it is done.

Nutrition: Makes 12 servings.
Each serving (1 square slice) has:

- 110.4 calories
- 12.8 grams protein

Rainy Day Soup—Crock-Pot

Serve this over cauliflower rice or just eat as is. Reheats well.

Ingredients:

- 1 pound lean ground beef
- 1 cup diced sweet onion
- 3 cups beef stock
- 1 (15 ounce) can fire-roasted diced tomatoes with garlic
- 1 (15 ounce) can tomato sauce
- 2 cups diced bell peppers (can use green, yellow, or orange)
- ½ teaspoon McCormick's ground oregano
- 1 teaspoon McCormick's Perfect Pinch Roasted Garlic and Red Pepper Seasoning
- ½ teaspoon McCormick's Italian Seasoning
- Freshly ground garlic salt, to taste
- Freshly ground pepper, to taste

Directions:

1. Spray skillet with nonstick cooking spray and heat to medium-high.
2. Brown beef in skillet with onions over medium-high heat.
3. Drain beef and onions and place in Crock-Pot.
4. Add all other ingredients to Crock-Pot and cover.
5. Cook on low for 8 hours.

Nutrition: Makes 6 servings.
Each 1-cup serving has:

- 177.3 calories
- 20.5 grams protein

Roasted Chicken Thighs with Zucchini and Feta

This is a tasty treat with a bit of a Mediterranean flair for a cool autumn night. It can be tossed together quickly and is enjoyed by all.

Ingredients:

- 1 pound boneless, skinless chicken thighs
- 2 medium zucchini, cut into 1-inch chunks
- 2 teaspoons olive oil
- 2 cloves garlic, minced
- 2 teaspoons dried oregano
- ¾ teaspoon sea salt
- ½ teaspoon freshly ground pepper
- Finely grated zest of 1 lemon
- ½ cup feta cheese crumbles

Directions:

1. Preheat oven to 425 degrees.
2. In baking pan, toss together all ingredients except feta cheese.
3. Bake for 20 minutes.
4. Raise oven temperature to 475 degrees.
5. Sprinkle feta on top of chicken and zucchini.
6. Continue to bake until chicken is cooked through and lightly golden, about 10 minutes.
7. Let stand for 5 minutes before serving.

Nutrition: Makes 4 servings.
Each serving has approximately:

- 221 calories
- 26 grams protein

Rotisserie Chicken, Spinach, and White Bean Stew

This is a quick and tasty way to use rotisserie chicken, chicken stock, and a few other ingredients to make a satisfying dinner to please the whole family.

Ingredients:

- 32 ounces chicken stock
- 12 ounces rotisserie chicken, chopped or shredded
- 1 (15 ounce) can cannellini beans, drained
- 4 cups baby spinach leaves
- 4 tablespoons pesto, for topping

Directions:

1. Pour stock into pot and heat over medium-high heat until thoroughly warm (almost boiling).
2. Add chicken, beans, and spinach.
3. Continue cooking until all ingredients are thoroughly heated through.
4. Place in bowls, top each with 1 tablespoon pesto, and serve.

That's all there is to it. Couldn't be any simpler, now could it?

PRO-TIP: You can preheat your oven to 175 degrees and place soup bowls in there to warm up. This keeps the food hot all the way to the last drop.

Nutrition: Makes 4 servings.
Each serving has approximately:

- 294 calories
- 34.5 grams protein (including pesto)

Salsa Verde Baked Shrimp

Pack these up and take them to work for lunches. A great grab-and-reheat meal, ready in a minute.

Ingredients:

- 1 pound shrimp, peeled and deveined
- 1 (12 ounce) jar Trader Joe's Salsa Verde

Directions:

1. Preheat oven to 450 degrees.
2. Spray baking dish with nonstick cooking spray.
3. Place shrimp in baking dish.
4. Pour salsa over shrimp and toss to coat.
5. Bake 18 minutes.
6. Use slotted spoon remove shrimp and leave excess salsa.

Nutrition: Makes 4 servings.
Each 4-ounce serving has:

- 131 calories
- 23 grams protein

Set It and Forget It Slow Cooker Turkey Breast

Set it and forget it! Save time and feed yourself delicious food with this recipe. Serve it with fresh veggies, a salad, or with your kiddos' favorite side dish.

Ingredients:

- 6 tablespoons minced garlic
- 1 medium yellow onion, cut into 4 chunks
- 1 lemon, cut in half
- 1½ pounds boneless, skinless turkey breast
- ½ tablespoon salt
- Generous amount of freshly ground pepper
- 1 teaspoon garlic powder
- 1 teaspoon onion powder
- 1 teaspoon sweet paprika
- 1 tablespoon extra-virgin olive oil
- 5 sprigs fresh thyme
- 3 sprigs fresh rosemary

Directions:

1. Spray slow cooker with nonstick cooking spray and be sure to plug it in.
2. Add garlic, onion, and lemon halves to bottom of slow cooker.
3. Place turkey breast on top of garlic, onion, and lemon.
4. Sprinkle turkey breast with salt, pepper, garlic powder, onion powder, and paprika.
5. Spoon extra-virgin olive oil over turkey breast.
6. Place fresh herbs on and around turkey breast as you see fit.

7. Cover and cook on low for 7–8 hours.
8. Once turkey is done, take it out of slow cooker. Slice and serve as you like.
9. Discard all herbs and veggies that were in slow cooker.

Nutrition: Makes 4 servings.
Each 4-ounce serving has:

- 232.5 calories
- 30.25 grams protein

Shanghai Shrimp and Crunchy Peanut Slaw

You can make the shrimp and eat them as is or combine them with the slaw. Both are yummy standalone meals.

Ingredients: Shanghai Shrimp

- 1 (12 ounce) bottle Lawry's Sesame Ginger Marinade
- 1 pound uncooked jumbo shrimp, with tail and shell on

Directions: Shanghai Shrimp

1. Add shrimp to ziplock bag and pour in marinade.
2. Marinate in fridge for 3 or more hours (even though bottle says 30 minutes).
3. Remove from fridge 30 minutes before grilling to let shrimp get to room temperature.
4. Set grill to medium heat and spray with olive oil.
5. Add shrimp to grill and discard remaining marinade.
6. Cook for 6 minutes, open the grill and flip shrimp, then close the grill and cook for another 6 minutes.
7. Remove from grill and serve with ½ cup Crunchy Peanut Slaw.

Ingredients: Crunchy Peanut Slaw

- 1 (16 ounce) bag coleslaw
- 2 cups shredded red cabbage
- ⅓ cup chopped green onion
- ⅓ cup red wine vinegar
- ⅓ cup vegetable oil
- 1 cup dry roasted peanuts

- 1 tablespoon water
- 2 packets Splenda (or your choice of zero-calorie sweetener)
- ½ teaspoon garlic powder
- ½ teaspoon seasoned salt (use Lawry's or Johnny's)

Directions: Crunchy Peanut Slaw

1. Combine all ingredients in large bowl and toss together.

Nutrition: Shrimp only—Makes 4 servings.
Each 4-ounce serving has:

- 210 calories
- 23 grams protein

Nutrition: Crunchy Peanut Slaw only—Makes 11 servings.
Each ½-cup serving has:

- 189.4 calories
- 5.5 grams protein

Shrimp Fried Cauli Rice

Cauliflower rice is a great substitute for rice in many recipes, saving you lots of calories and adding fiber. It works very well here in this take on fried "cauli" rice. You can certainly substitute chicken, turkey, steak, or pork for the shrimp, but be sure to adjust the calories. Family members from fourteen to seventy-one, love this dish.

Ingredients

- 1 pound raw shrimp, peeled and deveined
- 1 teaspoon sea salt, divided
- ¼ teaspoon freshly ground pepper
- 2 large eggs
- 1 medium onion, diced
- 5 green onions, sliced thin, with white and green parts separated
- 1 cup diced carrots
- ⅔ cup frozen petite peas
- 8 ounces fresh mushrooms, sliced thin
- 1 cup baby spinach, chopped
- 2 cloves garlic, minced
- 1½ tablespoons minced ginger
- 2⅔ cups cauliflower rice
- ¼ cup soy sauce
- 2 tablespoons rice vinegar
- 1 tablespoon toasted sesame oil
- Sriracha and Chinese mustard, optional

Directions:

1. Spray large deep pan or wok with nonstick cooking spray and heat to medium high. Season shrimp with ¾ teaspoon sea salt and pepper and add to pan. Cook shrimp, turning once, until pink. Remove shrimp from pan and set aside.

2. Remove pan from heat and spray again with nonstick spray. Whisk together eggs and ¼ teaspoon sea salt. Reduce heat to medium and add egg mixture to pan. Cook, stirring frequently, until eggs are done. Remove eggs from pan and set aside.

3. Add onion, white parts of green onion, carrots, peas, mushrooms, spinach, garlic, and ginger to the pan, mixing well. Cook until soft and tender, about 5 minutes.

4. When veggies are cooked, add cauliflower rice, soy sauce, and rice vinegar to pan, mixing all ingredients well. Allow to cook undisturbed for 2–3 minutes, then stir mixture thoroughly and allow it to cook another 2–3 minutes. Repeat this procedure until the "rice" has browned nicely throughout. This can take 10 minutes (but it is worth the wait as this process blends all of the flavors together).

5. Add cooked shrimp and eggs back to pan, mixing well until warmed through.

6. Drizzle with sesame oil and garnish with green onion tops to serve. Top with Sriracha and Chinese mustard, if desired.

PRO-TIP: Substituting boneless, skinless chicken breasts for the shrimp does not alter the calorie count, plus it increases the protein slightly.

Nutrition: Makes 4 hearty servings.
Each serving has approximately:

- 262 calories
- 34.8 grams protein

Shrimp Stuffed 'Shrooms

Use these 'shrooms to fill lettuce cups, or you can eat them with a fork or on a slice of whole-grain toast.

Ingredients:

- 7.2 ounces - 2 large portabella mushrooms
- 1 tablespoon Brummel & Brown Spread
- 2 tablespoons minced garlic
- ¼ cup diced yellow onion
- 4 ounces chopped bay shrimp
- 1 egg
- ¼ cup panko bread crumbs
- ¼ teaspoon salt
- ½ teaspoon pepper
- 1 teaspoon basil pesto
- 2 shakes Trader Joe's 21 Seasoning Salute
- 2 tablespoons grated Parmesan cheese
- Parsley, for garnish
- Lemon wedges, for serving

Directions:

1. Preheat oven to 425 degrees. Line baking sheet with parchment paper.
2. Remove stems from mushrooms and chop lightly. Place mushrooms stem-side up on baking sheet.
3. Melt butter in skillet on medium heat.
4. Once butter is melted, add chopped mushroom stems, garlic, and onion. Cook for 7 minutes.

5. Add in shrimp, egg, bread crumbs, salt, pepper, pesto, and 21 Seasoning Salute. Cook until shrimp and egg are cooked through.
6. Divide and fill mushroom caps with shrimp mixture.
7. Sprinkle 1 tablespoon Parmesan cheese on each mushroom.
8. Place in oven and bake for 15 minutes.
9. Remove from oven, sprinkle each mushroom with parsley. Serve with lemon wedge.

Nutrition: Makes 2 servings.
Each stuffed 'shroom has:

- 219 calories
- 19 grams protein

Sirloin and Lentils Skillet Chili

When you are tired and hungry, this is a fab go-to meal. Quick and delicious.

Ingredients:

- 1 tablespoon minced garlic
- 1 pound 93 percent lean ground sirloin
- Salt and pepper, to taste.
- 2 (10 ounce) packages Tasty Bite 1-Minute Madras Lentils (found at Costco)
- Optional toppings: cheddar cheese, sour cream, plain Greek yogurt, hot sauce

Directions:

1. Spray skillet with nonstick cooking spray.
2. Add garlic to hot skillet and sauté for 2 minutes.
3. Add sirloin to skillet; sprinkle with salt and pepper. Brown sirloin until cooked through.
4. Follow package instructions for lentils (can cook in microwave for 2 minutes).
5. Add cooked lentils to skillet with sirloin.
6. Combine well, reduce heat, and let simmer 5 minutes.
7. Top with cheddar cheese, sour cream, plain Greek yogurt, or hot sauce, if desired.

Nutrition: Makes 5 servings.
Each 5-ounce serving has:

- 261 calories
- 24 grams protein

Spicy Thai Grilled Chicken Thighs

The marinade takes about fifteen minutes to mix together, and we suggest marinating the chicken for as long as possible. While two to three hours will do, overnight is the very best.

Ingredients:

- 2 pounds boneless, skinless chicken thighs

Ingredients: Marinade

- 2 tablespoons fresh lime juice
- 1½ tablespoons chili paste
- 1½ tablespoons honey
- 1 tablespoon toasted sesame oil
- 1 tablespoon rice vinegar
- 1 tablespoon soy sauce
- 1 tablespoon olive oil
- 1 tablespoon minced fresh ginger
- 2 cloves garlic, minced
- ¼ teaspoon ground cloves
- ¼ teaspoon freshly ground pepper
- ¼ cup cilantro or parsley, chopped

Directions:

1. Add all marinade ingredients to bowl and whisk together to combine. If desired, reserve 3 tablespoons marinade for grilling (see <u>PRO-TIP</u>).
2. Pour into 1-gallon ziplock bag and add chicken thighs.
3. Close bag and shake, coating chicken with marinade.

4. Refrigerate for at least 2–3 hours or overnight, turning a few times to work marinade into chicken.
5. Heat grill to medium-high and grill each side of chicken for 3–4 minutes or until no longer pink. Discard the excess marinade.
6. Remove from grill and garnish with parsley or cilantro.
7. Serve and enjoy.

PRO-TIP: The nutrition values listed below include calories consumed if you use all the marinade. If you like, you can reserve some marinade from the ziplock bag before the chicken goes in and use it to brush the chicken while it's on the grill.

Nutrition: Makes 8 servings.
Each 4-ounce serving has approximately:

- 176.5 calories
- 22.3 grams protein

Split Pea Soup with Ham

This is a soup that will warm the tummies of the entire family while tasting great and meeting your protein needs. Leftover ham from a family dinner inspired this recipe, but you could just get a one-pound sliced ham from the market and have the same result.

Ingredients:

- 16 ounces dry green split peas
- 2 quarts chicken stock (or broth)
- 1 quart water
- 16 ounces cooked ham, diced
- 8 stalks celery, diced
- 2 cups diced carrots
- 2 medium onions, diced
- 2 cups zucchini, diced
- 1 clove garlic, crushed
- 1 teaspoon freshly ground pepper
- ½ teaspoon dried thyme
- 1 bay leaf

Directions:

1. Rinse peas in colander.
2. Add all ingredients to large soup pot and bring to a boil. Reduce heat and simmer for 3–4 hours or until peas are soft.
3. During cooking time, stir frequently.
4. When peas are fully cooked, remove from heat and allow to thicken a bit. Remove bay leaf.

5. If you like smooth soup, run small batches through your food processor or blender and add back to pot until the soup is your desired consistency.
6. Serve hot.

Nutrition: Makes 12 servings.
Each serving has approximately:

- 195 calories
- 18 grams protein

Sweet and Spicy Apricot Sriracha Salmon

Everybody loves contrasting flavors, and what could be better than sweet and hot wild-caught sockeye salmon? Pairs well with a side of asparagus.

Ingredients:

- 1 (8 ounce) sockeye salmon filet
- 2 tablespoons Smucker's Simply Fruit Apricot Spread
- 1 tablespoon Sriracha

Directions:

1. Preheat oven to 400 degrees.
2. Spray baking pan with nonstick cooking spray and place salmon in pan.
3. Mix together apricot spread and sriracha and then spread over salmon.
4. Bake for about 20 minutes or until salmon is just done (center flakes with a fork).
5. Remove from oven and serve.

Nutrition: Makes 2 servings.
Each serving has approximately:

- 205 calories
- 24 grams protein

WENDY CAMPBELL & SANDI HENDERSON

Zoodles and Zoodles of Shrimp

"Pasta" is back in our lives as either spaghetti squash or zoodles. *Zoodles* is short for zucchini noodles, made by using a Veggetti or similar tool to turn whole summer squash into miles and miles of noodle-like strands. These zoodles cook up in a flash and can be the base for any dish that calls for pasta. Whether using green zucchini or yellow summer squash the term Zoodles fits. This dish is delish.

Ingredients:

- 16 ounces yellow summer squash (also called crookneck squash)
- 8 tablespoons mango-peach salsa
- 4 tablespoons Herdez Guacamole Salsa
- 8 ounces raw shrimp, tails removed
- 1 ounce reduced-fat Mexican-style shredded cheese

Directions:

1. Make zoodles by running squash through Veggetti or similar device.
2. Place zoodles in 10-inch frying pan over medium heat. Cover and allow to cook for about 2–3 minutes.
3. Turn zoodles over, cover, and cook for another minute or two or until soft.
4. Remove pan from stove and drain. Set zoodles aside and keep warm (put them in a serving bowl and place them in a 200-degree oven).
5. Mix both salsas together and pour in skillet. Heat until salsas are just beginning to boil.

6. Add raw shrimp, cover, and simmer for about 2 minutes. Turn shrimp; the underside should now be opaque and pink. Cook for another 2 minutes or until just done.
7. Top zoodles with shrimp and salsa mixture, add cheese as garnish, and serve.

Nutrition: Makes 2 servings.
Each serving has approximately:

- 258 calories
- 24.8 grams protein

Connect with Us

Now that you know what we eat and how we plan meals with firm protein and fresh vegetables to keep us satisfied and optimize the results of our weight loss surgery, we invite you to become a member of the WLS Success Matters family.

There are several ways to get connected:

- Go to www.wlssuccessmatters.com for information about our online educational courses, one-on-one coaching, and free telephone support groups. No matter where you are on your journey or where you live, we are here for you.
- Follow us on Facebook: https://www.facebook.com/wlssuccessmatters/
- Find us on Twitter: @WLSSuccess
- Subscribe to our YouTube Channel: WLS Success Matters

You never need to walk your journey to health alone!

Made in the USA
Middletown, DE
06 May 2017